How I Learned to Like My Mom

Forgive Those You Love
... Before It's Too Late

Dorenda Doyle

ISBN: 979-8-9858908-2-2 (hardback)
ISBN: 979-8-9858908-1-5 (paperback)
ISBN: 979-8-9858908-0-8 (ebook)
ISBN: 979-8-9858908-3-9 (audio)
Library of Congress Control Number: 2022904967

Cover design by Cutting Edge Studio.
Printed in the U.S.A.

Thank you for purchasing *How I Learned to Like My Mom*. I would like to show my appreciation for buying my book with this free short story featuring my grandma!

In addition to this insider view of my grandma and her wisdom, I'll include a free copy of her recipe to make her amazing Homemade Yeast Rolls.

Visit www.PullUpYourBootStraps.org to get "Grandma," my short story, and claim your free gift today!

Thanks for reading!
Dorenda Doyle

To Sadie Jo Lowry Brown Stout McGee Buchanan:

"You kept our family together, Mom."

And to my brother, Rodney, and sisters, Jo and Taffy.

Bootstraps, LLC

PullUpYourBootstraps.org

Table of Contents

Prologue

The Mom I Loved but Didn't Like

"Angel Flying Too Close to the Ground" by Willie Nelson

Is there someone you *love*, but you don't particularly *like* ... even when you're *supposed* to? For example, what if that "someone" is one of your parents, maybe even your own mother?

Society, history, psychology, philosophy, and all the other "y"s out there tell us that all mothers are to be adored. So, of course, I *loved* the woman on my front cover—the one who gave birth to me, raised me as a single mom the majority of her life, tried to keep me safe, and loved me even when I was *really* unlovable. And, believe me, I could be plenty unlovable at times, especially in my teens.

But, I did not *like* my mother.

In fact, I spent my entire childhood and adult life *not liking* her. I barely tolerated her. I was embarrassed by her. I constantly judged her and found her lacking.

Before you think me a horrible person, let me explain. In a nutshell, my mother was a beauty who could never find love. Believe me; she tried ... She married SEVEN times! She drank too much and made poor life choices. Yes, I judged her. And, even worse, I judged myself as unworthy every time I recognized that I was like her in my own actions or thoughts.

This is an uncomfortable place to be, and I was in this uncomfortable state for most of my life. It was even worse once I realized just how *wrong* I was about my mother, that she wasn't as awful as I had thought. Regretfully, this insight came too late.

It was my mother's death that jolted me awake. I see that now. I see that I had been too wrapped up in my own hubris and self-righteousness. I see my own immaturity. Clearly, I see that she and I were too much at odds all my life to have met in the middle. And I see that she had been too proud to have shared her secrets. With all this hindsight, I see that although I loved her, I did not even KNOW her well enough to have liked her.

This book is my journey of finally getting to know my mother—her family history, her many husbands and boyfriends, her careers, her talents and faults, and ultimately, what all these factors meant to my siblings and me.

As an educator (now retired), I have always sought information in order to solve a problem. The problem, as I saw it, was that I still held resentment and unresolved issues with my mother; and now that she had died, I didn't know how I was going to fix it. Although I had ignored and avoided facing these issues for decades, it was obvious that they had taken a toll in my own relationships. Yes, it was time I learned as much as possible about my own mother.

What I found out about her is detailed within the pages of this book. I will tell you this: these details finally allowed me to focus and accept what had been right in front of me all my life, what Mom had demonstrated all *her* life:

- Love without judgment.
- Forgive unconditionally.

This lesson was the tip of the iceberg. I hope my process of discovery will encourage you to do the same for yourself and whoever it is in your life that you love but might not like.

Chapter 1

Why Read a Book About Someone Else's Mom?

"Mommy Is Sleeping" by Jo Stout

I was 61 years old when my mother died ... when I first consciously realized I had spent my entire life avoiding her as much as possible. Yes, I loved her, but I did *not* respect her. I most certainly didn't want to spend any more time around her than I had to. It took her death, and a *lot* of very reluctant self-reflection, to make me admit she "wasn't all that bad."

My first epiphany was the realization that I didn't give to her, that which she had *always* given to me and my siblings—unconditional, non-judgmental love and forgiveness. Talk about guilt and regret!

And, it was a very tough pill to recognize that I had *never* given my mother the appreciation she deserved, nor allowed her ever to think I valued her as a person. In fact, I finally admitted to myself that I had treated her with disdain, barely showing her a modicum of tolerance the majority of the time.

At this point, you may be thinking, "So, this story is to somehow make the author feel less guilty." True.

But it is also to wake up others regarding their own parents, or siblings, or whoever is in one's life that may be taken for granted. If I can help just one other person not to make the mistakes I made with my mom—before it's impossible to rectify—then all this effort will be worth it.

Besides her dying, what in the world made me start all this self-reflection? Well, I got saddled with the job of giving my mother's eulogy *(more on this in the final chapter)*. As one ages, few friends are still alive to give tributes. I was chosen by default.

I'm sure it had something to do with the fact that I have been an educator all my life, so my siblings thought I wouldn't mind speaking in front of a crowd. As I reluctantly agreed to do it, I realized there was no way I was going to give a speech without being prepared. And, as an educator, I have always tried to put a positive spin on everything— even a speech about a mother that I didn't particularly like.

So, I started digging into past photos, talking to relatives, and gathering memories from my siblings. I was determined to give my mother a positive send-off, focusing on the upbeat portions of her life.

Here's where it got sticky. The more I read or heard, the more I tried to put facts into some semblance of order, and the more I tried to relate the incidents of her life into an historical context, well … the more I realized I kind of actually *admired* this woman!

I will warn you, that when one embarks on a journey of discovery, it is oftentimes very painful. You see, I wasn't just uncovering facts about my mother's life; I was realizing truths about my own.

I had a lot of healing to do and didn't even know it. To heal oneself, one has to let go of resentment and find forgiveness. And, to find forgiveness, one has to face each of the perceived wrongs and look for reasons to forgive, to let go of the grudge.

In the months between her death and her memorial service, and especially in the years following, I came to appreciate this woman, her life lessons, even her questionable parenting. I began to forgive her mistakes. I have come off my high horse, realizing I, too, have made parenting mistakes—who am I to judge *anyone*? This was my own first step toward healing.

It is only in hindsight that my siblings and I have finally realized what a truly remarkable person Mom was ... and what a positive impact she made on our lives, as well as the lives of others. We have come to appreciate this marvelous survivor who overcame obstacles that would have leveled most of us, and overcame barriers that we knew nothing about. Yet, she always found a way to persevere.

Within the chapters that follow, I want to share what I learned about my mom and, thus, what I revealed about myself. I want my readers to see how my emotions evolved as I uncovered facts and as I opened my mind to learn as much about my mother as I could. It was, at times, hurtful and still is. There have been nights that I couldn't sleep because of memories that were dredged up. There were days when regrets and guilt engulfed me.

This is my mom's life story, but it is also partially mine. She spent a lifetime chasing love and happiness, never finding it because of her bad choices and life circumstances. However, she somehow supported four kids amidst her alcoholism, seven marriages, lack of education, and questionable morals. She never gave us up for adoption, never went on welfare, kept us out of the crosshairs of Child

Services, and taught us to always pull ourselves up by our bootstraps.

By today's standards, we think of horrible parents as drug addicts or gang members, but back in the '50s, a single mother was the pariah of society. And if that mother were beautiful, which my mom was, it was even worse. Growing up, my three siblings and I always thought she was one of the worst mothers ever.

Truly, until her death in 2015, I would have told anyone that my mother was a very poor parent, that oftentimes, I felt like the adult in the family, raising *her* rather than the other way around. I think my siblings would have said the same. In fact, I've purposely named each chapter in this book by a song title because, honestly, I felt like we were living the lyrics of an awful country song. There is one other reason I used song titles, but I don't want to give away that part of the story just yet.

My mother spent a lifetime teaching us lessons that I didn't value until it was too late to tell her "thank you." These are her unspoken teachings I want to share in the following chapters. Some of these lessons she taught by example, some on purpose, some by mistake, and some through her various associations—friends, family, or even husbands.

So, I ask you once again, is there someone in your life that you love but whom you do not *like*? If you lost that someone tomorrow, would you have regrets? Are you giving them non-judgmental love ... even if they are not reciprocating? Are you willing to forgive them unconditionally?

By sharing my mother's story and my own in the chapters that follow, can I somehow encourage you to:

1) learn more about that someone?
2) learn to accept them, including failures and fallacies?
3) learn to forgive their mistakes?
4) forgive *yourself* and them unconditionally?

Can you begin to *like* that someone as well as *love* them? Before it's too late?

I hope so ... I *sincerely* hope and pray so.

Chapter 2

Mom's Family

My research started with diving into our family tree. All but one of my aunts and uncles had passed or were bedridden, so I had to rely on stories from older cousins and family photos. Bless all the relatives who actually wrote on the backs of pictures—they provided a base for me to start building the facts of my mother's life.

So, let's start at the beginning ... my mom was the youngest of nine children.

Nine kids!?!? Are you serious!? Well, yes, back in the good ol' days, large families, especially those on farms, were definitely the norm. The theory was, the more kids, the more farmhands that didn't have to be paid. Plus, I'm not sure exactly when birth control was invented.

My mom, Sadie Joan Lowry, was the baby. I only ever heard people call her "Jo;" my grandmother was the only one who called her "Sadie Jo." Jo was born in 1928 in the little town of Hollis in Southwest Oklahoma. I am fortunate to have a baby photo of my mother, thanks to one of my aunts.

Figure 1 Sadie Jo Lowry, born April 12th, 1928.

For those of you who might not remember your high school history, this was about the time of the Great Depression (1929) as well as the decade of horrible droughts that became known as the Oklahoma Dust Bowl (1930–1940). As a result, my mom's family relocated to the so-called "Land of Milk and Honey," California, at least for a short time. And, to further complicate her youthful years—she would have been 17—WWII ended in 1945.

So, what do all these catastrophic world events have to do with my mother? I believe all these occurrences had a bearing on who and what my mother was. I don't exactly recall my psychology classes, but the "Nature versus Nurture" debate is still ongoing. In my mother's case, I believe her character was a result of both. How could it not have affected her personality, growing up in a period of food shortages, home and income losses, and mate deficiencies?

For myself, growing up as a baby-boomer, I thought the worst outside event that affected my formative years was the Vietnam War ... that is until COVID-19 hit the U.S. in 2020; it will be decades before we can look back and judge how this latest worldwide devastation has impacted our society or individual personalities. However, I am getting ahead of myself because I haven't even introduced my mom to you.

As I said, my mother, Jo, was the youngest of nine children, growing up on a farm in rural southwest Oklahoma. I have memories of my aunts and uncles, who were almost all much older than my mom, saying things like, "She was always Mom's favorite," or "She was always spoiled." Even my grandmother admitted that my grandfather "never said, 'no'" to my mom. I remember that my grandmother, Nerva (short for Minerva), seemed to always be there when my mom hit a rough spot, be it financial or emotional. However, it was also true that my grandmother lived with us the majority of my teen years up until her death, with either my mom or one of us kids taking care of her.

My Mom's Parents, My Grandpa and Grandma

I've already addressed the outside world events that may have shaped my mother, but what about her upbringing, her siblings, her parents? Let's start with her parents, Samuel Frank Lowry (1885–1959) and Minerva (Cosby) Lowry (1885–1979). Although born in different states (grandmother was from Illinois, grandfather was from

13

Texas), they both ended up in Oklahoma. The Oklahoma Land Rush took place in 1889 when they were only 4 years old, so this might have been how they came to be in the "Sooner" state.

According to the 1930 Census, my grandfather had only a fifth-grade education, referred to as "elementary school level" by Ancestry.com. My grandmother was credited with having a "high school education" because she had completed the ninth grade. One of the surprises I came across in my research was that my grandmother's younger sister, Sadie, married my grandfather's younger brother, Forrest. Two sisters married two brothers.

My grandparents married in 1905 in Greer, Oklahoma. They were "dirt poor" farmers with a small homestead in Hollis, Oklahoma.

Figure 2 My grandparents' home where my mom grew up.

Figure 3 Samuel Frank and Minerva (Cosby) Lowry, wedding photo January 3rd, 1905, Greer, Oklahoma.

I have no memory of the original farm but have strong memories of the home and small acreage they built "in town" once they got older and returned from California, which, evidently, did *not* turn out to be the land of milk and honey.

According to family legend, my grandmother was at least a quarter Native American; whether it was Cherokee or something else, that was always up for debate. I finally decided to check the validity of this family legend by doing a DNA test. (I didn't want to be another Elizabeth Warren.) Turns out, yes, we do have Native American in our ancestry, but how much or which tribe I do not know. This is not surprising since my family originated from the Southwest.

In today's current divisive climate of racism and emphasis on people "of color," I know my mom would be proudly claiming her Indian heritage. I look at it this way ... we are *all* people of color—I haven't met a clear-colored person yet. Why can't we all just claim to be part of the *human* race, focusing on our similarities rather than our differences!?

Figure 4 My Grandparents in front of the home they built in Hollis, OK, circa 1940.

Grandpa

I have three vivid memories of my grandfather, Sam. (Samuel—I don't think *anyone* went by their full name!) The first one occurred when I was about 3 years old, and my sister was only an infant. We were visiting my grandparents in their self-built concrete house in Hollis, Oklahoma. Grandpa was in his creaky wooden rocking chair, sitting by the upright furnace. He kept warning me not to get too close—yes, it had open flames. He was trying to teach me their telephone number ... Murray 8 5523. This was in the days when several neighbors shared a party line, and telephone numbers were preceded by a word. The "Murray" translated into MU or 68. I remember Grandpa being so very kind, patient, and rocking with me in that chair.

My second memory was of his protecting me from a so-called friend who turned out to be a pedophile (*more on this incident in a later chapter*). Regretfully, my only other memory of him was the blur of activity when they rushed him to the hospital right before he passed in 1959.

Grandma

My grandmother, on the other hand, has a permanent place in my very being. I have so many memories of my grandmother, I could fill a second book! She was my rock in an otherwise very shaky childhood. I used to say that any good traits I might have are because of my grandma and her influence on my life. If I thought my grandfather was kind and patient, then my grandmother was a saint! She was a never-ending source of wisdom and advice. I never once heard her raise her voice or get angry with my mother, no matter what the provocation ... exasperated, yes, even sorrowful, but never angry. I wish I had inherited or modeled my own anger management from my grandmother instead of from my mother.

She taught me how to play dominoes—and she was known to cheat once I got old enough to start beating her. I cannot count the number of games we played over the years. Once I got my driver's license, my mom would let me borrow her car—a metallic-blue 1970 Plymouth Duster—so I could drive my grandma from our house in Altus, Oklahoma, to her own house in Hollis, Oklahoma. This was a one-hour drive each way and gave me plenty of highway driving practice. Every once in a great while, we would stop midway to say hello to my Aunt Dollie.

Usually, though, my grandmother was in a hurry to get home. She would stay with us for a week or two, then return to her own home for another week or two. She had no television, only a little red boxy radio. Her light fixtures were electrical cords hanging from the ceiling with a light bulb plugged in. One such bulb hung over the dining table where we played dominoes. On the trips when I spent the night with my grandma at her home, dominoes was the only entertainment. My grandma's other favorite activity was reading the Bible, rocking in the very chair my grandpa used. The trips back and forth went on for several years until my grandmother's health started failing to the point that it was dangerous for her to live alone.

I once read that of our five senses, the sense of smell is the strongest in invoking memories. I believe that is true, because to this day, whenever I smell fresh yeast bread rising, I instantly recall my grandma, standing at the table, apron covered in flour, rolling out and pinching dough to make her fabulous rolls every morning until she was physically unable to do so. Although my cooking skills have improved with age, I'm afraid I did not inherit my grandmother's abilities. I will always credit her with my knowing what lard is, thanks to my helping her occasionally in the kitchen. And, no, you don't want that to be part of your daily diet.

I didn't realize it at the time, but my mother provided a template for me to follow in treatment of the elderly. She worshipped my grandmother and took care of her physically and financially when Grandma reached that stage of life when she needed help. Although Mom didn't always follow Grandma's advice or Biblical teachings, she did always show respect and at least listened. There is no doubt in my mind that Mom loved my grandmother deeply. Why I didn't learn this lesson—to always show respect and love to your own mother—I don't know.

Figure 5 My Grandma Lowry and her DELICIOUS yeast rolls.

Uncles and Aunts

I truly don't have a plethora of memories of every uncle and aunt, but I know their names and the order of their birth. All but my Uncle Dewey and Aunt Nerva Jewel were already grown and out of the house by the time my mother was born.

19

What follows is a synopsis of each, what I can remember personally or what was told to me as I grew up. Some of the stories were from my mom, some from my grandmother. From each of these nine Lowry children, I learned things, even if I didn't realize it at the time.

Uncle Cecil, Mom's Eldest Brother

Cecil L. Lowry (1905–1966) was their first child. As first-born son, he was expected to help my grandpa in the fields, and he most definitely did so. I faintly remember conversations between my grandparents where they referred to Cecil as "helping get the crops in." In a different time, my Uncle Cecil might have become a builder or an architect. He was instrumental in building my grandparents' home in Hollis, Oklahoma, as well as designing several buildings in California. He worked on a construction crew with my Aunt Fay's husband, Carl, in California.

Figure 6 Uncle Cecil, eating watermelon on the farm.

Figure 7 Uncle Cecil with Mom as a baby.

Aunt Dollie, Mom's Eldest Sister

Next came Aunt Dollie. Dollie Gertrude Lowry (1907–2001) was one of my favorite aunts, probably because she lived close to us as I was growing up. One of my BEST memories of her was stopping by her house once I learned to drive. She made a lunch for me that came entirely from her garden—big juicy beefsteak tomatoes, fried okra, green beans with butter, honied carrots, and of course, homemade hot rolls. Keep in mind she had to have been in her 80s at that time, but she was still tending her own garden, living by herself, and cooking for company. People always talked of my Aunt Dollie's hospitality. I filed these comments away in my head, wanting to be exactly like her one day.

One of my WORST memories is also of visiting my Aunt Dollie—she still had an outhouse until I was in my teens.

21

And, yes, we had to use pages from the Sears and Roebuck catalog—it was difficult to look at the yearly toy catalog after that experience.

Figure 8 Aunt Dollie and Aunt Fay as young women.

Uncle Loy, the "Rebel" of My Mom's Family

Loy Lester Lowry (1909–1979) was the next child of the nine. I suppose every family has a "black sheep," and Uncle Loy was always referred to as such. My mother was called "the wild child." The best I can recall, Uncle Loy earned the "Black Sheep" moniker because he was a drunkard. I do not remember ever having met or seen him, although I have met my cousins through his line—who are *not* drunkards! It's also my understanding that my Uncle Loy helped run a couple of speakeasies, including a bar or two owned by my great-uncle, Forrest (my grandfather's brother). Nowadays, such an occupation would not be frowned upon, but back in those days, I guess it was a mortal sin.

Figure 9 Uncle Loy.

Uncle Hubert, Business Owner, Mom's Favorite Brother

Hubert Lowry (1913–2002) was the third son born into the Lowry clan. Uncle Hubert opened an upholstery business that eventually became a chain of furniture stores in California, and he was characterized as being the successful entrepreneur and inventor of the family. One of his more famous inventions was some sort of lamp that had an aquarium circling around the light source. He sold it in his furniture stores—goldfish included—and received some awards and recognition for it, including being featured in a magazine and newspaper. He even had a patent for it.

Figure 10 Uncle Hubert with Mom in one of his first stores, Bakersfield, California.

He never let obstacles, be it financial or otherwise, stop him from achieving his dreams. He and my Aunt Alice, his wife, eventually retired to Fort Lauderdale, Florida. Uncle Hubert truly did find California to be the land of milk and honey, as did all his descendants. He, along with my other uncles, was a jokester and was always ready to tell stories and tall tales. Of all my uncles, I know he was my mother's favorite brother, at least once my Uncle Dewey passed away.

Figure 11 Uncle Hubert at Delray Beach, 1936.

Uncle Ray and Aunt Fay, the Twins

Twins run in our family, and my mom's next-born siblings were Opal Fay (1914–2016) and Jimmy Ray Lowry (1914–2002).

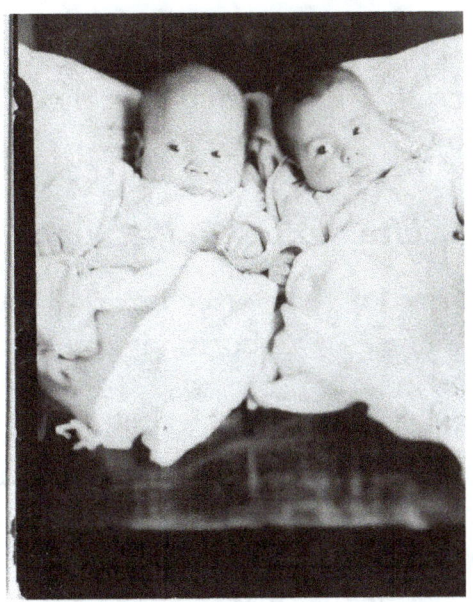

Figure 12 Ray and Fay Lowry.

Uncle Ray, the Story Teller Who Visited My Mom Often

I have lots of memories of both my Uncle Ray, in my early years, and my Aunt Fay, in my adult years. Uncle Ray was larger than life, telling jokes and stories and pulling pranks. If one of my siblings or I were pouting, he'd say, "Stick that lip out any further, and I'm gonna walk to town on it!"

I always loved for Uncle Ray to visit. For one thing, his son, Jimmy D, was my all-time favorite cousin … and as a preteen, I was enamored of him. Uncle Ray was married to Earlene. In one of the most difficult times of my young life, I wrote a letter to my Aunt Earlene, explaining in detail how

25

horrible my mom was, and telling her that I wished she, Aunt Earlene, were my mother. At the time, I had no notion of how to mail a letter, and my mom found it before I could figure it out. *That* got me in more hot water than I was already in!

This is one of those memories that has brought me great regret—how horribly I must have hurt my mother when she read that letter.

Aunt Fay, the Sister with No Patience for My Mom

Aunt Fay married a Tennessee boy and moved away from Oklahoma long before I was born. My childhood consisted of only three vacations—two of those were road trips to Taft, Tennessee, to visit my Aunt Fay, and one was all the way to Florida to do another familial visit. It was unheard of in the socio-economic level of my childhood to ever take a vacation unless it was a family visit. After all, visiting family meant a free hotel and free meals, at least for two or three days.

I always thought my Aunt Fay lived in the grandest house on the most beautiful land I had ever seen. She had a creek that ran through the property; Cold Creek was the name, green hills filled with livestock and woods that called for exploration. As a kid who had grown up in base housing, apartments, and trailer parks, it simply didn't get any better than this. I was also impressed with how spotless my aunt's house was. She was proud of her home, and the care she spent on it was noticeable. As a kid, I was amazed at her level of energy and industriousness. She was as active as one of us kids. If she ever sat down, it was only for a moment before she popped back up to do something else.

Figure 13 *Aunt Fay as a young woman.*

Once I became an adult and moved to Alabama, I reconnected with my Aunt Fay, who was still in the same house on the same land. I am thankful that my relationship with my Aunt Fay strengthened through the years; she provided the connection to my family that I had lost, mostly because of my own stubbornness. By this stage in my life, I myself had broken most ties with my mother, contacting her only on holidays. My Aunt Fay encouraged me to continue loving my mom and speaking to her, but to maintain a physical distance if for no other reason than my own sanity.

To this day, I treasure my visits with my Aunt Fay—her stories, her advice, and her spirit. I will be eternally grateful to her, my cousins, especially Sharrell and her husband Bill, and my second cousins, Terri and Tony (as well as Grady and Charlotte). They helped me through many difficult times—divorce, displacement, and even a hurricane! One of my best memories with this branch of my family was when they allowed me to help create a video for my Aunt Fay's 100th birthday. I learned so much history about my family with that project.

27

Aunt Fay lived to be 102 and still lived on her own until she was 101. Although I would like to claim to be as spunky as my Aunt Fay, I believe my younger sister, Jo, inherited her feisty and brave personality. This character trait served my sister well as she fought, *and won*, her stage 4 battle with cancer years ago.

Aunt Nerva Jewel, My Mom's Best Friend

Nerva Jewel Lowry (1919–2018) was closest in age to my mom. I believe there was an 8 or 9 year age difference at most. Throughout my mom's lifetime, she maintained the closest contact with Nerva Jewel, more so than with any other sibling. Oftentimes, it was a love/hate relationship—one of them would say something that ticked off the other, and phones would be slammed down. These episodes were quickly forgiven and forgotten. Of all my aunts and uncles, my siblings and I had the most contact with our cousins from this branch of the family, specifically her youngest daughters, Nerva Jo and Darlene.

Figure 14 Aunt Nerva Jewel and my mom, along with my mom's dogs.

28

This particular aunt had the greatest influence on my formative years. It is because of her that I became a Christian. She was my role model, along with Grandma, in showing me what faith truly is.

She is the only aunt with whom I ever spent the night. In fact, I spent a whole week with her one time so I could participate in a revival at her church. Aunt Nerva Jewel was what many would have called a "holy roller." She was the epitome of Saturday Night Live's "Church Lady" character. At least, this was true of her while she was still married to her first husband. In her later years, she became less strict but was always a devout Christian.

When I was a kid, I think she was thoroughly convinced I was possessed, and was always "laying hands" on me, casting out the devil. I am *not* exaggerating! Her daughter, Darlene, was between my younger sister and me in age but was years ahead of us in terms of precociousness. This is where the trouble stemmed; Darlene would instigate something, and I would somehow be left holding the bag. No, I wasn't nearly as smart or conniving as my cousin, Darlene. Of course, she is probably saying the same thing about me.

Figure 15 My mom and Aunt Nerva Jewel as young women.

Aunt Nerva Jewel was always considered the talented one of the family. She was an excellent artist, always painting or creating something. My mom used to say that I took after her because I had a gift for drawing, at least in my younger years.

I remember being so proud to call her when I was "saved" and baptized at the age of 14 at our little Baptist Church, Emmanuel Baptist, in Altus, Oklahoma. Regretfully, she was not kind in her response; I think she was too set in her opinion of me.

Uncle Dewey, a Gentle Soul Who Doted on My Mom

Dewey Hubert Lowry (1923–1963) was the youngest son, only five years older than my mom. I remember my grandparents were so proud of his being the first of their offspring to fully graduate from high school in 1943, even being a member of the Honor Society. Fate, however, had other plans for my gentle uncle. He joined the service shortly after graduation and fought in WWII. Regretfully, my only memories of him were while he was being kept in his bedroom at my grandparents' home until his death. Nowadays, he would have been diagnosed with PTSD, for he had violent outbursts, not knowing where he was or what was happening around him.

Figure 16 My uncle, Corporal Dewey Herbert Lowry, WWII.

Figure 17 Uncle Dewey with my mom before he shipped overseas.

31

Throughout my life, I heard all my aunts and uncles refer to my Uncle Dewey as a "gentle soul with not a mean bone in his body," always doing good deeds for others. It's a wonder he survived the war with this disposition, and really, he did not. My brother, Rodney, resembles Uncle Dewey in looks and character. And although I didn't really know my uncle, I think the two of them are kindred spirits because I would also describe my brother as kind-hearted, mild-tempered, and generous to a fault.

One of my favorite family photos is of my grandparents, my mom, and Uncle Dewey. I have no idea the year, but it had to have been before my uncle joined the service in 1945, so my mom was 17 or younger.

Figure 18 Sam, Nerva (grandparents), Uncle Dewey, and Sadie Jo Lowry (my mom).

My Mom and a Preview for the Rest of This Book

By the time my mother, Sadie JoAnn Lowry, their ninth child, was born, my grandparents were both 43 years old. When I think of this, I realize that I come from REALLY TOUGH stock. How in the world did my grandmother survive, let alone thrive, after giving birth at that age? I thought I was old when I had my own son at age 26.

Evidently, the women in my family have been gifted with longevity. My grandmother passed at age 94; Aunt Dollie was also 94; Aunt Fay was 102; Aunt Nerva Jewel was 99. Only my mom died "young," comparatively speaking, at age 87. I told my husband when he married me that he had better know what he was doing because we Lowry women live a *long* time, and he was going to be stuck with me! Luckily, this threat did not deter him.

I have only bits and pieces of stories from my mother's youth. I truly wish I had paid more attention. I know she always had dogs, and her all-time favorite was a Spitz named Snowball. She also loved horses.

Figure 19 Grandpa with Mom's dog, Snowball.

Growing up poor, she never had all the pretty clothes that her peers had. She, herself, told me that as a girl, she used to sit in the field on a tractor and pretend the spines on a hay thrasher were all hangers filled with one gorgeous outfit after another, all the clothes she would someday have. Although I, myself, would have described my mom as homely when she was a youngster, she was a gorgeous girl in her teen years and ultimately became a BEAUTIFUL woman, an asset she traded on frequently. Once grown, she was always well-dressed, well-groomed, and was never without a smile and a positive attitude.

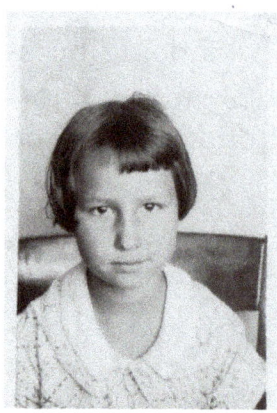

Figure 20 Sadie JoAnn Lowry, age unknown.

Figure 21 *Sadie Jo at age 13.*

Figure 22 *Sadie Jo, age 14 or 15.*

Figure 23 Sadie Jo, age 16.

She would occasionally mention a female friend, but it usually ended with a comment like, "she was jealous of me." And she frequently mentioned a barrel-load of boyfriends over the years, usually with the statement, "he cheated on me" or "he wanted to marry me." This became a repeating chorus throughout her life—more on this in Chapter 3.

Figure 24 Sadie Jo (back row, 3rd from left, holding doll) approx 7–9 years old with Holsmith girls—Mary Loyd, Gracie Lu, Glenna, Lorene, Alta Pearl, and Frances.

According to one of the Ancestry.com documents, my mom received no further education beyond the fourth grade (1940 Census), but I would dispute that. My mother was well-spoken and had excellent grammatical skills, so she had to have received a good level of education by the time she quit, whatever the grade level was. She always told us that she quit school after the eighth grade; I never did hear why. I don't know the time frame, so I don't know if they were in California or still in Oklahoma when this happened.

Figure 25 Sadie Jo (2nd row from bottom, 4th from left) 4th and 5th Grade, Mrs. Nichols' Class, La Casa School in Harmon County, Oklahoma.

She never considered education important, however. Nor did her lack of a degree ever stop her from getting a job. Of course, the jobs were not "good" jobs, but at least they put food on the table. Chapter 4 details the many careers of my mother.

Mom was not only a "looker" throughout most of her life, she also had more than a little talent for writing jingles and songs. Despite her having looks and talent, things always seemed to fall apart before she could ever catch the big break. Her many highs and even more lows are chronicled in Chapter 5.

Because my grandmother was such a wonderful person, one would expect my mom to have made a terrific parent. Instead, my siblings and I often felt that we were the adults in the home. It was by the grace of God that at least three of us kids turned out fairly decent. More specifics on this in Chapter 6.

My mother made friends easily. She could talk to anyone and had a genuine interest in others ... even if that interest was fleeting, and was only there to establish what my mom could gain from the interaction. Somehow she engendered loyalty from people, and I mean people from EVERY walk of life, and from EVERY economic level. I've detailed some of these relationships in Chapters 5 and 7.

Figure 26 Sadie Jo with Wanda (Pete Lowry's sister).

I don't think my mom could have been a Lowry without some of the familial traits rubbing off on her. Yes, she had a sense of humor. Yes, she was quirky. Yes, she always found the silver lining in every cloud. And, yes, she NEVER gave up. Lots of stories, which exemplify these traits, are covered in Chapter 8.

Family was always important to her, and she would have walked through fire for any member of her family, especially us, her children, in spite of her poor parenting decisions. As painful as it is, I explore this aspect of her life in Chapter 9.

Figure 27 Sadie Jo and Grandpa Lowry at the old home place in Hollis, Oklahoma.

Figure 28 Sadie Jo with Grandpa and Grandma Lowry.

Finally, in Chapter 10, I explore my mom's legacy of love and forgiveness, and what it means to my siblings and me.

Lessons I have learned from my mom's family:

- Watch out for the little ones; give them your time and attention. (Grandpa)
- Forgive easily; don't hold a grudge. (Grandma)
- Always help your family. (Uncle Cecil)
- Be hospitable and welcoming to all. (Aunt Dollie)
- Do what you must to make a living; it may not be what everyone else approves of, but it puts food on the table. (Uncle Loy)
- Be willing to look at the funny side of any situation, even if the joke is on you. (Uncle Ray)
- Be energetic and enthusiastic in all you do. (Aunt Fay)
- Never give up on your dreams or accept your present circumstance as unchangeable. (Uncle Hubert)
- Avoid being judgmental. (Aunt Nerva Jewel)
- Have faith in your own talents and abilities, and especially in God. (Aunt Nerva Jewel and Aunt Fay)
- Be kind whenever possible. (Uncle Dewey)
- Family is forever; it is your #1 priority. (First lesson taught to me by my mom)

As I look back, I realize some of my first life lessons were being taught by my mother and her siblings, as well as by my grandparents. I hope this chapter has nudged you to think about your own family or circle of friends. Every soul we encounter in this life can have a positive impact—let's hope we have an affirming effect on others.

Now, the REAL reason you probably picked up this book was to find out if it were true that someone, other than a movie star, could possibly have been married *seven* times. That answer is awaiting you in the next chapter.

Chapter 3

Mom's Seven Marriages

"DIVORCE" by Tammy Wynette

I thought about entitling this chapter, "Of Mice and Men," but that just didn't seem appropriate. Or maybe "The Many Marriages of Jo," or even, "Lucky Number Seven!" In the end, I decided not to embellish this fact about my mother any more than necessary.

Seven Marriages, huh? Yep! Or at least, those are all the marriages my siblings and I are aware of. Before I delve into each of these soap operas, let me explain something ... none of us are completely sure when my mother was born. To the best of our knowledge, and my research on Ancestry.com, my mom was born in 1928. I am basing that on the 1930 Census record, which indicates Sadie J. Lowry was "1 ½." Okay, my math is not THAT bad ... I know this would mean my mom was born in 1929. However, on further research, I found that the 1930 Census date was April 1st, 1930. IF my mother were born in 1928, she truly was NOT 2 years old yet (birthdate of April 12th). This hypothesis is further supported by the fact that none of the other Lowry children listed in the 1930 Census had a "1/2" by their age. I'm also basing the 1928 birth year on the recollections of my mom's sisters: my aunts.

So, what's the big deal—1928 or 1929? Well, to further complicate things, throughout my mom's life, she lied about her age. Why, I don't know, because she was gorgeous at every age, but perhaps it had to do with the ages of her husbands or boyfriends. When I was in my late 20s, which would have put her in her 50s, my mom introduced me to a boyfriend who was in his 30s—told you she was gorgeous.

In addition to stretching the truth about her age, my mother changed the dates on photos or other documents. You'll see evidence of this on some of the photos I've included in this memoir. For the most part, she claimed to have been born anywhere from 1932 to 1942.

Perhaps my mom lied about her age because my grandmother *may* have done the same thing. In one section of Ancestry.com, my grandmother's birthdate shows to be 1883, so she would have been two years older than my grandfather. In the 1930 Census, she is listed as four years younger than my grandfather. In the 1940 Census, she is listed as five years younger than my grandfather. Finally, in several Ancestry.com records, she has a birth year of 1885, same as my grandfather. I know, back in the day, it was a vanity thing for the wife to be younger than the husband. Perhaps that is the reason for the discrepancies. At any rate, I'm just fine with my husband bragging that I am a Cougar, or that I robbed the cradle—I am 6 months older than he is.

The reason for all this diatribe on age is this: all our lives, we were told she first married at age 14 and had my brother by age 15 ... thus, the reason she had suffered such a rough existence and had made such poor marriage decisions throughout her life. I suppose she thought we, her kids, would somehow be more sympathetic if we understood what a bumpy start she had experienced as a young woman. I don't know what effect it had on my siblings, but I, for one, was dead-set against sex or marriage until I finished college. So, if that were my mom's intent—to scare us straight—it certainly worked for me!

From the many photos I've obtained, I think my mom had a pretty active dating life, both before and between her marriages. Reading between the lines, I believe my mother was fairly precocious at a young age. When I analyze it, she had elderly parents—they would have been in their late 50s to early 60s when she hit her teens. So, perhaps they were too tired to monitor her as closely as they should have.

Once upon a time, I could not have related to this, but now that I am in my 60s, I *cringe* to think I'd have to raise a teenager. My oldest granddaughter is a teenager, and I cannot begin to try keeping up with her. I simply grin and act like I know what she's talking about when she carries on about TikTok or SnapChat or whatever else is the latest craze; she's a fantastic young lady, and as much as I love her, thank God, she's her parents' responsibility, not mine. So, I can definitely understand why my grandparents might have been less than attentive or even aware of what my mother was doing.

Plus, my mom learned very early how to "stretch the truth," and my grandfather was especially susceptible to her charm. Over the years, I've been told by various aunts and uncles that my mom had the gift of a silver tongue. That is double-speak for saying that my mother prevaricated a *lot*. She carried this trait throughout her life. Even my sainted grandmother often said, "Sadie Jo will lie when the truth is easier." So, lying about her age was NOT the first or only fib my mom ever told.

As a young person, even before my teens, I learned not to fully trust what my mother said. Somewhere I read that habitual liars don't even know when they lie, that the lie becomes "a truth" in their own minds. So that's how I was able to cope with my mom's lack of veracity—I often excused it by saying, "that's how Mom *wishes* it were."

My mom's tendency to lie definitely made a mark on me. To this day, I will blab *everything* just so I can't be accused of lying or withholding information. I would have made a terrible spy! Whenever someone starts a conversation with, "now, don't tell anyone..." I immediately throw up my hands and say, "NO! Don't tell me if you don't want it repeated! I can't keep any secrets!!" This makes for very interesting gossip sessions, I can tell you.

Over the years, my mother had a plethora of beaus; some were hometown "heroes," and some were from the local air base. Altus Air Force Base was only an hour's drive from Hollis, where my mom lived. And, I'm fairly sure that a young woman with little education and even less money saw an airman as a perfect escape route out of her podunk birthplace.

Figure 29 Sadie Jo with SSGT Travis Jr. Brown, circa 1941–42.

Figure 30 Sadie Jo and Junior Sorrells, taken January 2nd, 1953, in Hollis, Oklahoma.

Figure 31 Sadie Jo with unknown beau.

I have to make a lot of assumptions about my mother's relationships with the opposite sex because I don't have a lot of facts, and there were a *lot* of exaggerations regarding marriages, boyfriends, dates, and divorces. I had *some* photos directly from my mother, but most of those had dates altered. And, as unlikely as it sounds, my mother had *two* house fires that totally destroyed everything—the first occurred in Maryland before I started school. The second occurred many years later in Oklahoma after I had married and left home. (*More on these two catastrophes in My Final Words.*)

Thus, the majority of the photos in this memoir were gifted to me by my aunts, and even some cousins. I treasure each and every one. Altogether they provide tattered pieces of my mom's life.

Marriage #1, Clinton Stanley Brown (1924–1979), Father of My Brother, Rodney

Figure 32 Sadie Jo with her fiancé', Stanley Brown, circa 1943, before he joined the Navy.

In spite of dating mostly airmen, my mom's first husband was in the Navy. And, unlike the tall tale she always gave us kids, she did *not have* to get married at age 14. Turns out, my mom married her first husband, Clinton Stanley Brown, at the age of 17, and he was 21. According to the newspaper article, the ceremony took place in California on April 25th, 1945.

Sadie Jo Lowry Is Married To Clinton Stanley Brown

Miss Sadie Jo Lowry, daughter of Mr. and Mrs. Samuel Frank Lowry of Lawndale, California, formerly of Hollis, was married to Clinton Stanley Brown, S 1-c, son of Mr. and Mrs. C. L. Brown of Hollis, formerly of Wellington, on April 25. The ceremony was read in the Marriage Manor at 3201 West Pico Blvd., Los Angeles, with Rev. Julius Du Bose officiating.

The bride wore a wedding gown of white satin fashioned with a full skirt and a sweetheart neckline and short sleeves. Her halo was of white and a short fingertip veil was attached. For something old she carried her mother's white lace handkerchief and something borrowed was a strand of pearls. Her corsage was of white gardenias tied with a blue satin ribbon.

Attending the couple were Mr. and Mrs. Samuel F. Lowry and Hubert Lowry.

Mrs. Brown had made her home in Hollis until a few months ago when she moved with her parents to Lawndale.

The groom attended school at Wellington. He entered the Navy in November 1943 and is serving on a cargo ship. He has just returned after spending 10 months in the Pacific.

The couple plan to make their home in Hollis after he is out of service.

Figure 33 The Wellington Leader (Wellington, TX) July 19th, 1945.

The article also states that my mom "had made her home in Hollis (Oklahoma) until a few months ago" before she moved to California with my grandparents. One would assume the two met in Southwest Oklahoma since Stanley lived in the area as well.

Figure 34 Stanley and Sadie Jo Brown Wedding.

He was a Specialist 1st Class in the Navy and had recently finished a tour of duty in the Pacific; he had joined the service at age 19 and received an honorable discharge in November 1945, only a few months after their marriage. Not sure what occupation he had after his stint in the service, but his death certificate at age 55 indicated he was a paint and body worker in the automobile industry. His short military career might have been a root cause of the failure of their marriage; hearing stories, again from aunts and uncles, Stanley had a lot of oats to sow, and his cheating was not tolerated by my mom. Again, who knows what really happened ...

Figure 35 Stanley and Mom, possibly an engagement photo or post-marriage.

Stanley, as we always knew him, was the father of my brother, Rodney, my oldest sibling. Rodney was born in 1948. Obviously, I have no memory of this first husband, but we heard that he "broke her heart" and "cheated on her with her best friend, Trixie." I'm reminded of a poster I once saw: "If a man expects a woman to be an angel in his life, he must first create heaven for her. Angels don't live in hell."

Figure 36 Mom with Rodney, at approximately 1 year of age.

I could find no record of their divorce, but I assume it was by 1951 because that's the date my own father, husband #2, stated was their marriage year.

Whatever year they divorced, my mother did not find being a young divorcée with a toddler son to be a deterrent to her social life. I found a number of photos of my mom with various men; some even included my toddler brother, Rodney. Even without my brother in the pics, I know these took place after her marriage to Stanley Brown because my mom wrote "Jo Brown," along with the guy's name on the back, and sometimes, the location.

When cleaning out my mom's house, my sister and I found a small, well-worn photo album. It was filled with pics of men, some with notes on the side. There was Eugene Dickenson, a Navy officer, courting her in Hollis, Oklahoma. Johnny Freeman from Eldorado, Oklahoma, was supposedly her "fiancé" at one point. Richard Morris must have lasted a good while because she had numerous pics of him; he even posed with my brother, Rodney, in several photos.

Figure 37 Boyfriend, Richard Morris, holding my brother, Rodney, after Mom divorced Stanley.

Donald Ray Thompson appeared a few times as well. Dude McCubbin looked to be a candidate for husband #2 since there were lots of pictures of him with my mother. I lost count of how many nameless photos of servicemen were included in her album; perhaps she dated some of them, perhaps not. Maybe she was sowing her own wild oats as was her first husband, Stanley.

As it turned out, all these men were passing fancies because she waited until my own father appeared before remarrying again.

Marriage #2, Joseph Howard Stout (1929–2014), My Father

Figure 38 Joseph Howard Stout, my father.

In her kinder, less guarded moments, my mom would wax poetic about her courtship with my father. According to her, he pursued her hard and asked her to marry him on their second date. What amazes me about my dad falling so hard for my mom is that she had already been married and had a young son, my brother, Rodney. I don't think he *really* understood what he was getting into … a ready-made family.

Figure 39 My dad, Joe Stout, in uniform, with a newborn me, and my brother, Rodney.

Figure 40 My dad, Joe Stout, me, my brother, Rodney, and Trixie, our dog.

I've read one letter that my dad sent to my mother, and wish I still had it. It was written within the first few years after they married (1951), and my dad had already been deployed overseas. My mom was back home, living with my grandparents, my brother, Rodney, in tow. I was non-existent, I think, because I was never mentioned in the letter. I remember being so glad to have found the letter because my memory of my parents' marriage was one of constant conflict, discord, and an overall feeling of unhappiness from everyone. But, the letter told a different story. I believe my dad genuinely loved my mom, at least in the early days of their relationship. In the letter, my dad repeatedly called my mom loving terms—Sweetheart, Honey, my Darling.

However, I definitely caught the main gist of that particular letter—it wasn't one in which he professed his love or loneliness and how much he missed them, although these were mentioned. Primarily, he cautioned my mom to try and live within a budget, that he had no more money to send home. Since I have no notion of his salary at the time, or how much he was sending to my mom, let alone how much it was costing her to live and support a baby, I cannot fault either of my parents. I choose to believe that my mother was doing the best she could, perhaps even supplementing my grandparents' income since she was living with them, *and* I choose to believe my father was sending every spare dime home to his new wife and stepson. He even held extra jobs like working at base NCO Clubs after hours. And, it wasn't as if my mom were sitting doing nothing; she was also trying to hold a job, in spite of her lack of skills or education.

Like my mom, my dad came from a large farming family; he was the oldest of eight children—three sisters and four brothers. However, as the oldest, he worked the farm as if he were an adult; my uncles told me that my grandfather was an extremely hard taskmaster. "Joe was expected to be in the field before sunrise, and had better not have shown his face at the house until after sunset."

Regretfully, it was from this man that my dad learned his parenting skills, such as they were. As a result, my dad was intolerant, hard, abusive, and unforgiving as a parent ... hardly the qualities needed in a new marriage with a young stepson who had had no real male role models. Some of my worst memories of this time in my life were when my dad beat my older brother, who could not have been more than 10 years old, to the point that Rodney had to go to the hospital for stitches and concussions. Remember, this would have been the 1950s, and "disciplining a child" was accepted and tolerated. If this happened today, my father would have been arrested, and my brother might have been taken into Child Protective Custody. I truly hate that this was the role model for my brother and that he was made to suffer in any way. By the Grace of God, my brother came through this and is the best, kindest father, as well as the Godliest man I know.

My dad was never abusive to me or my sister, Jo; if he beat my mother, I have blocked that memory, but I don't recall my mom ever mentioning it.

I will **never** excuse or condone child abuse, but I do realize my dad was raising Rodney as he had been raised. Sorrowfully, my dad forgot that this type of raising was exactly what made him leave home to join the service the minute he turned 17 and finished high school.

Figure 41 My Family circa 1956.

Since I've shared the most awful character trait that my dad had, I would like to take the time to share some of the best of my father. He had an illustrious 20-year career in the United States Air Force, traveling all over the world, and retiring at the rank of master sergeant in 1968. He once told me that, "in the service, you have the salary of a pauper, but you travel like a king." I'm pretty sure my own travel bug is genetically linked to my dad. His work career continued with a 25-year stint as a postal carrier for the United States Post Office, retiring in 1989.

But, he didn't stop there ... until he retired for good in 2004, my dad spent fifteen years as a manager for Edwards Theaters. Even once he retired, my dad created works of art in the form of cross-stitched paintings that were so realistic they looked like photographs. He was definitely a workaholic (another trait that I have from both him and my mom), but he was also very creative, devoted to his siblings, and loved the outdoors. I did not learn about most of this until I became an adult because it was my mother who raised my siblings and me.

After my parents divorced for the final time around 1963, I saw my father once more in 1965, and never again until 1974. There were no letters, phone calls, or contact whatsoever. I blamed my mom for this, but in reality, both parents were to blame.

Figure 42 Rodney and me, Easter 1956.

This brings up a very important point: since divorce is so prevalent in our society, it is extremely imperative that parents *not* denigrate the missing parent to the child. The child hears all these terrible things about their mother or father, and starts to think, "Wow, I'm the product of these two horrible people—that must mean that I am horrible!" I can tell you first-hand that when this is how you are raised, you grow up with a sadly-lacking self-worth. It can also cause the child to choose relationships and spouses that repeat the cycle. The child's ability to judge wisely is greatly hampered.

Marriage #3, Jerry (Last Name Unknown)

Figure 43 Jerry, husband #3.

The separations due to deployments, the lack of money, and the immaturity of both my parents led to their first divorce—after my birth in 1954. I have photos of my being held as an infant by my dad and one when I was about a year old. I can find no records, so I guess the divorce had to be around 1955.

I also have photos showing that my mom, my brother, Rodney, and I returned to Oklahoma, presumably again living with my grandparents. I know that my mother dated a number of men after divorcing my father, based on dated photographs.

According to my mother, it was during this time that she met "the love of her life." Jerry was in the Navy. My mother once showed me a photo of a very handsome man with blond hair in a Navy uniform, and told me that Jerry was the only man she had ever truly loved. She also told me that their marriage lasted only a few months because he had been killed. She never told me how he died. And, I've never been able to confirm with other relatives the veracity of that story.

Marriage #4, Joseph Howard Stout, My Own Father Again, and That of My Sister, Jo

My mother reunited with my father sometime in 1956, with my sister, Jo, being born the next year. This was officially my mom's fourth marriage.

As an Air Force family, I can remember living on the base in Ft. Meade, Maryland. I know that I started grade school there, at least my first-grade year. Mom was a stay-at-home mom, making ends meet with various "acceptable" outlets (*more on this in Chapter 4*) that befit a non-commissioned officer's wife. During times of my father's deployment, we were required to leave base housing and live in local apartments or rental properties. These were not always pleasurable surroundings.

Figure 44 The Stout Family, circa 1960, Jo, Joe, Sadie Jo, Dorenda, and Rodney.

Once my sister, Jo, came along, it seemed for a little while that our family might make it. She was named after not only our father Joe, but also my mother, Sadie Jo. Jo was the shining star in our family; her optimism and sweet personality were like a Disney character come to life, and still is. In all our family photos of my dad, my mom, my brother, Rodney, and myself, Jo is always the one smiling and happy. I truly do not remember her *ever* misbehaving, talking back, or disobeying my parents. She simply wasn't that kind of kid. As a result, while growing up, I was so jealous of her I couldn't stand it. It was, as a young adult, that I recognized what a treasure she is, and she is definitely my very best friend. Despite hundreds of miles of separation, we talk every day.

So, another important point: no two kids are ever completely alike, no matter how they are raised in similar environments. Give each one a chance to shine and value whatever positive traits are exhibited.

Despite some maturity having been gained by both my parents, my dad's bad temper, his continued absences, and my mom's disillusionment with love and her own life goals led the marriage to dissolve again around 1962. My mom and her now three kids all moved back to Oklahoma, while my dad continued with his Air Force career. If any letters were exchanged, they were never shared with me. Nor did any of us ever receive a birthday or Christmas present from my dad. Again, his raising reared its ugly head. My paternal grandparents were devout Jehovah's Witnesses and therefore did not celebrate such holidays. This was so very opposite to my mother's upbringing, where her family would celebrate the slightest event. So, no contact occurred, and my father slid to the back of all our memories, only to be resurrected on occasion when his child-support check was late.

Thankfully, I was able to reconnect with my dad in 1974 as a young married adult. Initially, my mother was very angry at me for reestablishing a relationship with my father, but she got over it. Perhaps she finally realized that I needed that part of my existence resolved in order to move forward with my life. I was able to meet my half-sister, Angelika, whose mother, Heidi, had met and married my father when he was stationed in Germany. When my own son was born in 1981, I wanted him to know both sets of his grandparents, just as if we were a "normal" family. I was naïve enough at that time to believe there really was such a thing. Now, I'm pretty sure abnormal is the "new normal."

In-Between Marriages

So, it's around 1962, and my mom would have been 37, still a prime beauty who had never lost her figure. I assume she had ample opportunities to remarry, but I seem to recall that her child support from my father would have terminated if she had done so; perhaps it had something to do with his being in the military. I don't think that's the way it works these days, but it was certainly the stricture she operated under back then. That income, as sparse as it might have been, was sometimes all that put food on the table, especially since my brother's dad had never paid any support.

That did not stop my mother from having a full social life, mostly men she had met at the air base where she waitressed at the NCO Club or at the bars where she worked as a barmaid. Numerous pictures of various men fill an old scrapbook. Some of the names I recall—Kenneth Chambers was mentioned often. If we ever met any of these particular men in person, I do not remember. I think my mom *tried* to keep her social life separate from her family life.

We lived very frugally, most always in low-priced rental houses that were, as Mom put it, "just this side of the bad part of town." These houses had no frills, such as air conditioning. Believe me, summertime Oklahoma hits triple digits! But, because we had a dog, Mom made sure there was always a fenced backyard; so we, kids, had plenty of play area. And, despite working full-time, and sometimes even an additional part-time job, Mom kept our home absolutely spotless. No matter how hard she worked, there were times when extra money was needed, and my mom's bar tips were not making ends meet. Tires on our car, a refrigerator going out, lots of things could throw Mom's meager budget out of whack.

Therefore, a handful of times, Mom announced, "Pickin's are slim," and she would make a road trip from where we lived in Altus, Oklahoma, back to Hollis. These trips were *never* taken when my brother was home, but always during the daytime when it was only my sister, Jo, and me. I would have been in second or third grade, I think, fourth grade at the most. My mom would arrive in Hollis, stop at a phone booth, and make a call while my sister and I sat in the car. The calls didn't last long; then, she'd get back in the car and drive to some remote dirt road outside of the little town of Hollis. There would be another car parked there, alongside the road. Mom would pull up about 30 yards behind the vehicle and warn my sister and me, "do *not* get out of the car" and "do not look toward the other car." As I got older, I started asking questions:

"Who is in that other car?"

"Why are we meeting that man?"

"What is his name?"

My mom informed me at some point—I could be unrelenting in my need to know, including being sneaky and rolling down the window so I could hear her phone booth conversation—that she was "meeting an old friend" who would give her some money to help out with things until her next paycheck. It was never very much, a couple of twenty-dollar bills at the most. The man's name was W.P. She had to meet him in secret because he was 1) married and 2) some bigwig at a bank or something with a reputation to uphold.

From my child's eyes, he was a fat dirty old man, and I hated that my mother let him kiss her—as I said, I was sneaky, and being told "don't look" only made me strain my neck further. As an adult, I know my mother was doing what she had to so we could pay bills and eat. Perhaps there are those among you, who read this, and condemn her for these adulterous meetings, especially with two young daughters in tow.

Figure 45 W.P., not a husband (at least not to my mom).

But, I think my mother knew exactly what she was doing. By having her daughters with her, the pawing and kissing couldn't go further than that, and could never last longer than five or ten minutes. Again, as a child, I had a child's sense of the passing of time. If any of these visits had lasted longer than five or ten minutes, I probably would have gotten out of the car and investigated. My mother knew this, and probably counted on it.

The bottom line was that she used this "fine upstanding citizen" as much as he used her. I think Mom came out the poorer for it, as it stripped away her dignity. We would drive away from these clandestine meetings, stop at the nearest gas station, buy a Coca-Cola, and my mom would take a swallow, swish it around, and then she immediately spit it out. My sister and I got the remainder of the Coke. A win-win for us, plus my mom had money to go buy groceries.

As far as I know, my brother never knew of these episodes with W.P. He, however, had his own demons to fight regarding my mother's escapades. Between Mom's marriages, my brother thought of himself as the "man of the house," the "protector of his mom and sisters." What a burden to have placed on the shoulders of a young teen.

It had to have been one of Rodney's worst memories, the night he had to face a grown man who had followed my mom home to our trailer house. The Pink Elephant Club was adjacent to the trailer park where we lived. My mom sometimes worked there, sometimes partied there. On this particular night, Mom had had too much to drink, and as she stumbled in, a total stranger tried following her into her bedroom. Rodney stood up to him, a man twice his size, and probably as drunk as my mother was. My memory may be blurry, but I remember a scuffle, a lot of yelling, and threats on the part of both adults. I was told to call the police. My brother was finally able to shove the guy out our front door before we locked it.

Before you turn skeptical on me, I *know* a flimsy locked trailer door, let alone a skinny teenage boy, would not have been a deterrent to a full-grown man if he had really wanted to pursue my mother into her bedroom. Perhaps the threat of the police call, as well as three screaming brats, did the trick because we had no further trouble from him.

Marriage #5, Bob "Parker"

Sometime around 1963 or 1964, Mom met and married a guy named Bob. My sister, Jo, doesn't remember him at all. My brother and I have debated over his last name, but the consensus is that it was Parker. Rodney recalls that he was an officer in the Air Force, a lieutenant, he thinks. I recall that Bob was from Colorado. Neither of us remembers Bob having ever even spent the night at our trailer home. I think Mom and Bob went across the state line into Texas and eloped on a whim. The whim didn't last very long because Bob did *not* like any of us "brats," as he called us. The marriage was doomed when Bob insisted that Mom leave us with someone so they could go skiing in Colorado, meet his family, and have a proper honeymoon. Anyone who ever knew my mom *knows* that we, kids, *always* came first. She would never have left us. So instead, she left Bob. No loss as far as we, kids, were concerned.

Marriage #6, Alvin James "Chick" McGee (1927– 1994), Father to My Youngest Sister, Taffy

Mom married Chick, Alvin James McGee, in 1964 or 1965. He was a non-commissioned officer, a sergeant, I think, at Altus Air Force Base. Mom met him, as she did most of her beaus, at the bar or club where she worked, in this case, the NCO Club of Altus Air Force Base. Chick was a chef there, and my mom was a waitress. She had my youngest sister, Taffy, in late 1965, and he seemed to be a devoted father.

Figure 46 Mom and Chick McGee with newborn Taffy, my youngest sister.

Despite being a functioning drunk, Chick was a decent provider. It was during this marriage that my family finally purchased a house, the only home I ever lived in as a child that wasn't base housing, a trailer, or a rental. I remember that my Aunt Nerva Jewel, as well as my grandmother, liked Chick; he was the first good wage-earner my mother had ever married.

That's about all the good I can say about this man. He was abusive when he was drinking, which was all the time. I had to call the MPs (military police) more than a couple of times because he attacked my mother. One incident, in particular, stands out, where he was choking her against a wall; she passed out, and we kids thought she was dead. Whether it was this incident or an accumulation of several, my mother's throat continued to give her problems throughout her life. It sometimes closed up on her to the point that she couldn't swallow anything but liquified foods.

Chick's and my mother's favorite pastime was drinking or bar-hopping. By this time, my brother, Rodney, could babysit us when my grandmother was at her home in Hollis. I tried to always be in bed, dead asleep before they returned, because it was usually a knock-down, drag-out fight when they walked back into the house. Accusations flew, as did beer bottles, until one or the other passed out.

Figure 47 Chick and Mom, between fights.

I did not trust Chick to ever be alone with him or to leave my sister, Jo, with him. He was a little too "handsy" and used every opportunity to touch us as we matured. Mom was still married to Chick when I met and ultimately married my first husband in 1974. I was attending the local junior college in Altus. Unlike many of my peers, I did *not* marry in order to get away from home, but I was certainly glad to be leaving all of this turmoil behind.

Innately, I knew that a good education was my ticket out, not a guy. I was determined never to be dependent on a man for my well-being. This was one of those lessons my mother inadvertently taught me by example—her life was a series of "what not to do" in relationships. I equated her lack of education with her failure in marriages and careers. As I look back, I realize other factors contributed to these failures, but as a young adult, lack of education seemed to be the best reason. As a result, I've always loved learning, and even now, in my 60s, after achieving post-graduate degrees, I continue taking classes whenever possible. Mom, who never seemed to value education, attended all my graduations where I actually marched. She would never have admitted it, but I believe she was proud that I had chosen an academic path.

Figure 48 Chick with my sister, Jo, and me.

I don't know when Mom's marriage to Chick dissolved, but none of us mourned its loss.

Figure 49 Chick and Mom, not long before they divorced.

A side note on Stanley Brown (husband #1 in case you have lost count and needed a reminder): Mom actually dated him *again* after divorcing Chick, maybe around 1974 or so. I'm not even sure my brother knows about it. But there is photographic proof.

Figure 50 *Stanley Brown (husband #1) with Mom, circa 1974, Texas.*

Marriage #7, Harold Lloyd "Buck" Buchanan (1927–2008), First Husband My Mom Buried

My mother married the first truly decent man (not counting my own father, who, let's face it, wasn't a great prize with his temper) on December 26th, 1975, in Childress, TX. She was 47.

Figure 51 *Chief Master Sergeant Buck Buchanan, my mom's last husband.*

Buck was a chief master sergeant at Altus Air Force Base. If my mother met him at a bar, I'd be surprised; I never once saw Buck take a single drink. Buck had been married before as well and had two grown sons. I met them occasionally through the years, but honestly, I selfishly never bothered to get to know them better; I figured this marriage would also be short-lived. I was wrong. Mother stayed married to Buck until his death in 2008.

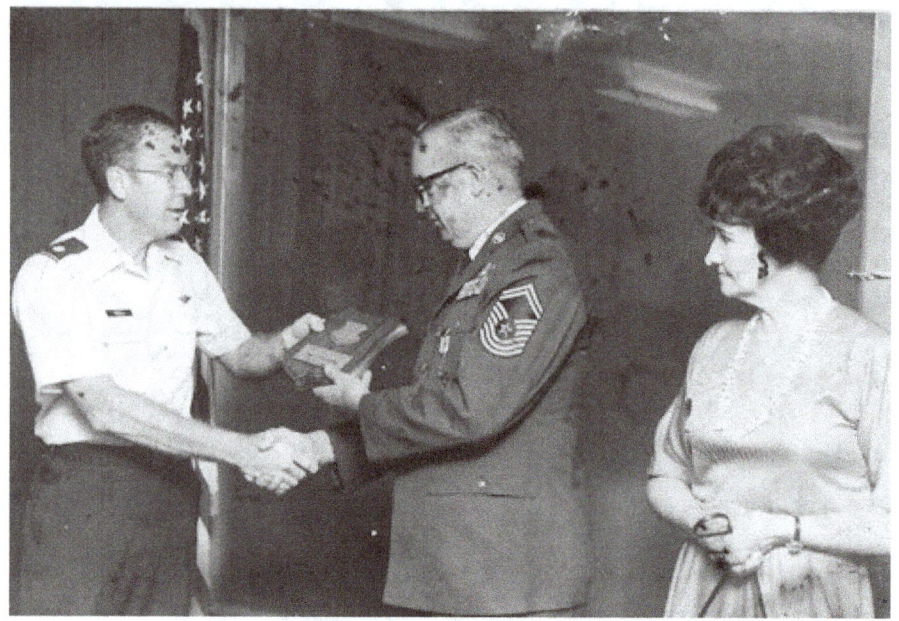

Figure 52 Buck and Mom at his Honorable Discharge Ceremony.

After being honorably discharged from the Air Force after 30 years of service, Buck went to work as a civilian at the base, creating curriculum for the C-5 cargo plane. Serendipitously, I was a curriculum writer for a school system in Lawton, Oklahoma, as well as for the State Department of Technical Education for Oklahoma. Buck asked me to come to the base as a consultant at one time to share the methods I used to develop curriculum and learning materials.

I didn't realize at the time what an honor that was, and it was much later that I grasped how very proud Buck had been to claim me as his stepdaughter. In fact, I distinctly remember his introducing me as his daughter; it was a bit disquieting because I never considered him my stepfather, let alone my father. In my mind, he married my mother after I left home, and I was married myself, so why would he have even bothered to acknowledge me in any way? It was a new experience for me to have one of my mother's husbands actually want to claim me. After that, I always referred to Buck as my stepfather. To this day, I regret that she didn't meet and marry this man many husbands earlier.

Figure 53 Buck as a civilian, working as a curriculum writer for the C-5 cargo plane training.

I had never heard of the Masonic Lodge, except in movies, before Buck, but he had been a member for 50 years, even serving as a past Worshipful Master of the Altus Chapter. He was also a member of the VFW, the American Legion, the

Scottish Rite, the Officer's Club, and the NCO Club. The only clubs any of my mother's other husbands had been members of were the ones that served beer or whiskey.

Figure 54 Buck in later years at a Masonic Lodge event.

Initially, Buck was a good influence on Mom; if she didn't stop drinking, she at least slowed it down, and she stopped her bar-hopping days. He was a quiet man, deliberate in his actions and speech. When he married Mom, my youngest sister, Taffy, was 10 years old. He even adopted Taffy a couple of years into their marriage.

I blissfully lived sixty miles away from Mom and Buck. I was newly married and focused on finishing college, starting my career in education. In other words, I was so caught up in my own life, that I was totally unaware of what was happening in my mother's home. I wanted to believe Mom had finally found a good husband, and some happiness; I didn't bother to confirm by calling or visiting … Why borrow trouble? I *should* have done so.

By the time she was 13, my youngest sister was already headed down a path of self-destruction. And Taffy's destruction led to the ruin of the only good marriage my mother had ever had.

As she aged, Mom's behavior began deteriorating, and she exhibited as little control over my sister as she did on her own temper and language. Each time I went for a visit, the yelling, cussing, and name-calling was unbearable, escalating as the years passed. She and Buck were horrible to each other, at least verbally. I do not believe that Buck was ever physically abusive as Mom's other husbands had been, but the verbal abuse between the two was intolerable. It literally made me a nervous wreck, and I often pulled over on the side of the road to throw up when I left to return to my own home.

Even though we only lived about an hour away for most of the years, I never once spent the night in my mother's home after I left in 1974. By the time my own son had been born in 1981, I wanted nothing to do with my mom or anyone in that household. Yes, I made the requisite phone calls and sent the expected cards and presents through the years, but that was about it. I abandoned not only both my sisters, but a man that I truly might have loved as a stepfather had things happened differently.

As I look back, it is amazing that my two sisters even acknowledge me. I essentially abandoned them. Today, my sisters, my brother, and I have a very strong relationship, and love one another deeply. It speaks strongly of the lesson we all learned from my mother: Family is forever. We forgive and forget.

This I also know: I will *never* abandon any of my siblings ever again. And, I know for a fact that all three of them would come to my aid in a New York second.

Figure 55 Buck and Mom in their short-lived twilight years.

Buck and Mom were married 33 years when he died in 2008, but it was NOT a happy marriage or a happy household.

Lessons Learned from My Mom's Many Marriages

Growing up with a revolving door of men and marriages, I was dead-set against getting married, *ever!* My mom didn't ever need to worry about my getting drunk or pregnant while I was in high school. But, I did eventually fall in love my second year of college, not with any of my classmates, but with a blind date set up by one of my college friends.

Looking back, I know I fell in love, not only with my son's father but with his family. His mom and siblings, as well as his grandparents, aunts, and uncles, were everything I had always wanted—a cohesive family unit with no divorces and lots of solid family traditions.

Every Sunday, the entire clan would meet at his grandparents' farm bringing all kinds of dishes. Between aunts and uncles and siblings, there were at least twenty family units with dozens of kids—my favorite kind of people—running around. The whole Sunday was spent eating, visiting, joking, and playing outside. I absolutely *loved* it! I had never experienced anything like it, other than my Uncle Ray's occasional visit. *This* was the "Leave it to Beaver"/"Father Knows Best" kind of existence that I yearned for—good wholesome gatherings with no cussing or drinking. I probably decided to fall in love with my first husband based solely on that initial Sunday. To this day, these gatherings are some of my favorite memories; I regret that my own son was born too late to have participated.

Of course, nothing stays the same. As the grandparents passed, and some divorces occurred as well as devastating illnesses, this wonderful family tradition bit the dust. My own marriage dissolved after 21 years.

When my son's father told me he no longer loved me and wanted a divorce "before I hate you," I agreed.

Let me rub more salt into the wound. I did *not* get an attorney. I did *not* fight the divorce. I did *not* want my son to go through what I had as a child—the bickering, name-calling, dragging-through-the-mud fiasco. I didn't even ask for child support *(yes, "stupid" was stamped on my forehead)*, let alone alimony.

You see, I was still wearing rose-colored glasses, and I was *determined* that I would stay married, no matter what.

I was *not* going to follow in my mother's footsteps. I kept telling myself that my husband was going through mid-life crisis, that he would wake up and realize what he was throwing away. Even after the divorce was final, I was pathetically thinking he would change his mind.

The bottom line was that I was *in love with the idea of a lasting marriage.* But truthfully, I was no longer in love with my son's father. I think a full year passed after the divorce before I suddenly woke up and recognized this fact. And it's a bit sobering to realize that the fault of the divorce wasn't strictly that of my first husband … it's on my shoulders too, because he surely felt that I didn't love him. In hindsight, it was an unhealthy relationship for us both; two basically good people were bringing out the worst in each other. I believe he was an unhappy person, and I couldn't fix it.

One of my favorite people in the world is a former boss, and now most definitely one of my dearest friends—Abbot Marcus Voss of Saint Bernard Abbey in Cullman, AL. I'm not Catholic, but I was employed as a teacher at Saint Bernard Prep School before my first marriage ended. I remember being so scared to tell Fr. Marcus that I was getting a divorce. After all, everyone knows Catholics don't sanction divorces, so I was afraid I was going to get fired.

Instead, after explaining the whole Catholic stand on this issue, and assuring me that I was *not* going to lose my job, Fr. Marcus shared his view on marriages: the whole world is made of people that fit into two categories—givers and takers. The best marriages are made of two givers because each one will always try to put the other first. Regretfully, when a marriage is made up of a giver and a taker, the taker will expect the giver to solve all the problems and to do whatever is necessary to make them happy.

It's kind of an unspoken bargain. At first, the giver is all too glad to do this; after all, giving is what makes a giver happy. Eventually, though, the giver gets tired of this because it never seems to be enough; the more the taker gets, the more they want. This doesn't make the taker a bad person; it's their nature. From the taker's point of view, if the giver wants to back out on the deal, well, that makes the giver wrong because they are changing the bargain. Thus, this type of relationship is doomed for failure. Fr. Marcus thankfully put me in the category of giver; he's known me for almost 30 years, and I don't think he's changed his opinion of me. (And, Abbot Marcus, if you ever read this, please forgive me for paraphrasing your marriage discourse or misquoting you.)

In a nutshell, multiple divorces in one's childhood can have one of two devastating effects on a kid—either they will choose never to marry, or will choose to stay in a toxic marriage or relationship simply to prove they made a good choice. And, I guess there is a third option—multiple divorces, just like good old Mom and Dad.

For the longest time, I put myself in the first category; I was not inclined to ever remarry. So much so that I dated my current husband for nine years before we said vows in 2004. The fact that our middle-school-aged sons introduced us to begin with, also helped me overcome my aversion to a second union. Over the past 26 years, I've learned several things about marriage, or any long-term committed relationship:

- Successful marriages are the result of a four-letter word. *Love*, of course, is important, but the four-letter word I am talking about is **work!** You have to *work* at the marriage, at the relationship. It's not easy to hold your temper, to always speak kindly, to have patience, to put someone else first, to look for the good in your spouse on a daily basis. There really is wisdom in the Bible verses in 1 Corinthians 13:4–8.

- YOU are responsible for your own happiness. Even if your personality falls into the "taker" category, you can't expect anyone else to make you happy. That is surely the recipe for unhappiness.

- No one is perfect, and if you think the person you marry is, I'm afraid you are already doomed for failure.

- If you are more realistic and see that your spouse has faults, but you think you can change them, again, you are courting disappointment. I once heard a marriage ceremony in which the officiate said the success of the couple's marriage was much like their attitude toward the aisle and the altar:

  o If you think, "I don't like such and such about my spouse, but after we are married, it can be 'altared,'" then that marriage doesn't have much hope.

  o But, if you think, "I don't much care for such and such about my spouse, but 'aisle' learn to accept it, and hope that they will accept my own foibles as well," then *that* marriage has a chance.

- *Never* yell at your spouse unless the house is on fire … or they are about to hit the car in front—yes, I am a back/front seat driver. Also, it goes without saying, but I will anyway, *never* cuss your spouse.

- Neglect the whole world rather than each other.

- Stand united and be consistent when raising kids, even after they are grown.

- Try to see your significant other as others see them; be proud of them and their accomplishments; be their best advocate; be complimentary at least once every day; always show respect to one another, especially in front of others.

- Be responsible for your own actions; do nothing and say nothing that you wouldn't do or say in front of your own mother.

- Choose a mate that brings laughter in your life; in fact, I would say this is the #1 quality to look for! Looks will fade, money can be lost, but laughter will live forever.

- Never give up hope, on yourself or on a lasting relationship. I regretfully did not learn all these lessons in time to save my first marriage, but I'm surely trying this second time around.

Mom was indirectly responsible for anything I might have done right in my relationships. After all, she definitely was the poster child of "what not to do."

But it wasn't always what she *didn't* do. It was also what she *did* do. What follows are some of the lessons she demonstrated to us throughout her lifetime, in regards to her relationships:

- She showed us loyalty.

- She showed us optimism. If marrying *seven* times isn't an optimist, I don't know what one is!

- She showed us always to protect your kid, never to put a relationship before your own child's welfare.

- She showed us how important it is always to maintain one's own health and appearance as a sign of respect for one's partner. (And, if my husband Jimmy is reading this, do *not* count what I look like first thing in the morning!)

- She showed us hope; she never gave up hope for romance or true love.

Not sure where each of my readers is in terms of relationships, but hopefully, some of these lessons and advice will help.

And, if marriage and relationships aren't your thing, but careers are, then this next chapter should brighten your day. I would be willing to bet that no matter what job you have, the following account will make you feel *really* good about your own occupational situation.

Chapter 4

Putting Food on the Table

"9 to 5" by Dolly Parton

I'm about to give another history lesson, so please bear with me. Remember, my mom was born a year before the Great Depression and landed smack dab in the middle of the Oklahoma Dust Bowl, both figuratively and literally. Most all of her mate choices were drafted into WWII. She quit school by the eighth grade, and this *may* have been because her family had relocated to California. I will never know exactly why or how, but the result was a young woman with no education, no skills, and no way of making a decent living at a decent job. The United States was gearing up for, and then fighting, WWII. No wonder my mother was looking to land a husband, and preferably one that would take her away from a poor dirt farm.

However, let's look at some additional historical facts that may have contributed to my mother looking for a man to help support her. My mom, on her own, could not get a credit card or any kind of loan in her name—not because she had poor or no credit, but because businesses didn't extend credit to women. Not until 1974 was that law changed.

She could not open an account with the local utility company to turn on electricity or gas unless it was in her husband's or father's name. *That* practice was still happening even in 1995, at least in Cullman, Alabama.

When a man had no skills or job, he could always join some branch of the service. My mother couldn't have joined the service herself unless she had been trained as a nurse or secretary—sorry, they didn't teach any of those skills in the eighth grade. And, even if she had completed high school, she would not have been accepted into an Ivy League college until 1969 or later.

As I detail some of the jobs my mom held over the decades, I am very sad to realize how many times she was sexually harassed or discriminated against. I recall a number of times her talking about "This A-hole thought I'd go to bed with him just because I work for him!" or "Just because I'm a waitress doesn't mean that piss-ant I work for is going to paw me all over!" However, *none* of this was grounds for legal action until 1977.

I'm pretty sure health insurance was the last thing my mother worried about while trying to support four kids. However, if she had been financially able to buy health insurance, she would have had to pay more than her male counterparts, at least until 2010, when sex discrimination was outlawed in the health insurance industry.

Because of the struggles I witnessed my mom going through to support four kids while trying to work, I decided to postpone having a child until 1) I was fairly sure my marriage was going to last, and 2) I had finished college and had a career going. My mother did not have that luxury. Birth control pills were not legal until after 1960 in most states, and even then, only for married women.

I grew up during the Feminist decades and the fight for equal rights; I even experienced discrimination in my own early career, in the '80s. However, I never really understood what an *unfair* world my mother lived through until I sat down to write this memoir and started putting her life experiences on a historical timeline. How she survived and provided for all four of us kids without ever going on welfare or putting us up for adoption ... Well, I swear it makes me see her in a whole new light. I do *not* think I am or ever will be as strong a person as she had to have been.

With all that said, I'd like to briefly highlight as many of my mom's jobs as I can recall, and perhaps the impact they had on our family through the years.

Dr. Eargen's Medical Office

I wish I could find a Hollis, Oklahoma telephone book from the 1940s so I could correctly spell the name of Dr. Eargen (it was pronounced "Yeargen"), but this is my best guess. This was the first job I ever heard Mom talk about. She worked as a receptionist for Dr. Eargen for a few years, between her first and second marriages.

It's my understanding that after she divorced Stanley, she and my toddler brother, Rodney, returned to Hollis, Oklahoma, to live with my grandparents. I even have a letter that my Uncle Dewey sent to one of my aunts in which he states, "Sadie Jo and Rodney went to visit Nerva Jewel for a bit. Mom and Dad sure need the rest."

In the late 1940s, my grandparents would have been well past retirement age, but because they were self-employed farmers, they were not eligible for the social security benefits started in 1935. In fact, the 1935 Act only covered workers in commerce and industry. So, I am sure another two mouths to feed put a severe strain on my grandma and grandpa. My Uncle Dewey served his country in WWII but returned home with mental issues, which precluded his working anywhere, let alone on the farm with my grandfather. So, it would have been necessary for my mother to find work.

It is also worth noting that at the time, Hollis was a "one-horse" town with very little to offer in regards to employment; I don't know what it's like today. I believe Dr. Eargen gave my mom a job, to begin with, so she could pay for my brother's doctor visits, plus he was a good friend of my grandfather. There was even talk for a little while that he would train my mother as a nurse.

I don't know what went wrong, but my mom's career as a medical office receptionist was short-lived. Perhaps it was her own restlessness, but I strongly suspect it was more because the male clientele increased dramatically when my mom started working there.

From the point of view of the fine Hollis ladies, this was not to be tolerated. Besides her lack of skills, my mother was scandalously divorced! She had a kid! She came from honest, but let's face it, *poor* dirt farmers, not upstanding members of the community! And, worst of all, she was a *Beauty!* Why, she might steal every husband around, for God's sake!!

You might think all of this is supposition on my part, but I assure you, I have a first-hand witness. Believe it or not, one of my own first jobs while working my way through college was as a secretary in a school system for a gentleman who came from Hollis. Although several years younger than Mom was, Fred Emmert knew my mother, heard the rumors, and concurred that it was simply "a bunch of old jealous biddies" that cost my mom her first decent job. Regrettably,

I heard similar versions of this story throughout my mother's lifetime.

Dr. Eargen didn't just give my mother the boot. Instead, he recommended her to another doctor in the area, Dr. Allgood. I am *not* making up that name, I promise. Dr. Allgood was our family doctor for many years, so I absolutely know he was real. (But, a *great* name for a doctor, huh!?) My mother might have stayed working in that office until she retired, except my dad came along.

Maryland Housewife

My dad was stationed at Altus Air Force Base when he and my mom first met and married. I have no recollection of when we moved to Maryland, but that is where my dad was primarily stationed in between overseas posts. My dad was not an officer, so his pay was minuscule. Even though he took second jobs to help ends meet, it would have helped the home's finances if my mom had held a job.

Again, local prejudices came into play, as well as cultural mores. In the 1950s, wives were not supposed to work. For one thing, that would be competing for jobs that should be given to men returning from the war. For another, "decent" women were housewives, taking care of hearth, home, kids, and hubby. In addition, local businesses were not interested in hiring wives of servicemen because "as soon as I train one, she's leaving with her husband for his next post." This last sentiment was still prevalent in the 1970s when I first started looking for jobs.

But as a kid, I didn't see any of this. I selfishly wanted my own mother to be just like June Cleaver of Beaver fame or Jane Wyatt in "Father Knows Best," and for a while, she was. She wore heels and dresses every day. She attended PTA meetings and made cookies for different events. The house was spotless, inside and out. For anyone who has ever lived in base housing, this is a major requirement; commanding officers even held inspections of one's home occasionally.

What went wrong? I have only bits and pieces of clues. I think finances were the biggest obstacle. I know that moving in and out of base housing whenever Dad was deployed was expensive, even though my mom always returned to Hollis or Altus if he were stationed overseas. At the time, I always wondered why my mother and we, kids, didn't go with my father. It wasn't as if we were in a permanent home or school in which my mom thought we should stay. In fact, I lost count of the number of schools I attended from first to twelfth grade.

In retrospect, I *know* why we never went with my dad. He never adopted my brother, Rodney. So, even though the military would have paid to relocate my mom, me, and my sister, they would not have covered Rodney. There was no way my mom would have left Rodney, and I absolutely do not blame her.

Sometimes when my dad returned, base housing wasn't available. Then it was apartments or rent houses, and for our budget, these were often less than desirable. I don't recall my mom having any vices at the time, such as smoking, spending too much on clothes or jewelry, or anything for that matter. She certainly didn't drink at that time in her life. We lived pretty frugally. My brother would have been a tween at that time, not even a legal age to work; however, he *did* work—mowing lawns, raking leaves, shoveling snow, delivering newspapers—anything where he could help bring in money. I know he was trying his best not to be "some other man's burden." Yes, I remember those words being spoken by my dad as he complained about having to raise and pay for anything for my brother. It's no wonder my mom eventually filed for divorce and moved back to Oklahoma.

Waitress

It seems that waitressing is always the job that unskilled, uneducated people fall back on. What most people don't realize is just how hard this job is—on your feet for 8–10 hours at a time, few breaks, lousy pay, no guarantee of tips, customers that blame the waiter/waitress, rather than the cook, when they are unhappy with the food, and of course, lechers that see a waitress as somehow available to serve them more than food.

My mom was a waitress for more restaurants than I can count—local diners, Young's Café in Hollis, the Friendship Inn in Altus, the NCO Club at Altus Air Force Base, to name a few.

And don't equate waitressing skills with cooking skills. Although my mom could cook adequately—her spaghetti was her best dish—it was a family joke that she would put onions in our cereal if we didn't keep an eye out.

Growing up, we loved counting my mom's tips when she came home from a shift. Either she had already taken out all the dollars, or she didn't get any because it was only change that was poured out on the coffee table for us to count. It was a great way for a kid to learn math skills, I promise. I even learned how to roll coins before I turned 10, which was a very useful skill later on in life when I taught Banking and Finance.

Those tips were vital to our welfare. The minimum wage was 40 cents in the 1940s, up to 75 cents in the 1950s, and a whole dollar in the 1960s. If those wages weren't bad enough, keep in mind that these minimums were for non-restaurant workers only ... A restaurant employer was allowed to pay whatever they wanted, "as long as the tips plus the wage equaled the minimum of the time." This was known as the "tipped wage," and it has its roots in racism and sexism. (See OnLabor.org, "The Tipped Subminimum Wage.") Even in 1991, the tipped minimum wage was $2.13 while the "real" minimum wage was $4.25. To this day, I sometimes feel the need to educate friends at a restaurant when one remarks, "Well, I don't tip because the minimum wage is already so high." Most people, unless they have been employed in the restaurant industry, are completely unaware that wait staff are dependent on tips to bring their hourly salary up to minimum wage. So, YES, we were thrilled when my mom's purse was heavy with coins.

One other perk of my mom's waitressing was her bringing home food on occasion. I was a very picky eater, so I can't really recall what all she brought home, except for Gumbo. That was Chick's famous dish that he made at the NCO Club, where he and my mom worked. I hated it ... Still can't believe anyone would eat something that has fish eyeballs!

Barmaid

Being a town next to an air base, Altus had an excess of bars and honky-tonks. And being a very good-looking woman, my mom had an excess of job opportunities to be a barmaid. I didn't know until I was grown that these bars rarely actually paid any wages to the barmaids—they were expected to earn their keep with tips only.

The barmaid jobs were necessary when my sisters were too young to go to school because my mother had to be home during the day; a bar job enabled her to work at night while my brother or grandmother watched us. Besides, we were sleeping, so what could go wrong!? I know, Child Services would have a stroke these days.

But my mom held these types of jobs even once my sisters started school to supplement her other daytime jobs of waitressing or working as a maid.

Mom felt guilty about leaving us at night. On the nights she had to go to work before we got in from school, we would each find a comic book—my favorites were the Classics Illustrated—and a candy bar. Sometimes, it would be a dime for a Coke and a nickel for a Winner Sucker. It was always some treat we could look forward to because Mommy wasn't going to be home.

The tips were even more exciting from the bar jobs; it seems that drunks are better tippers than eaters. However, we never got any food from the bar. Those days, I don't think they worried about setting out nuts or pretzels or providing tapas. One of my worst memories of lean times was living in a trailer house, opening the refrigerator after school, and finding nothing but pats of butter in a little tray that Mom had brought home from her waitress job. To this day, I enjoy a thin slice of butter between two saltine crackers. I guess it reminds me to be grateful for never being hungry.

I was never embarrassed about my mom working at a bar until I was in the fourth grade. We were given an assignment to make a poster of an example of homonyms. Easy-peasy, right? However, I was an overachiever at school because it was the one place where I could get positive recognition. I didn't want to do a poster of some easy words that everyone else would probably choose—eye and I, ball and bawl, your and you're, to name a few. Oh, no, I wanted to choose words that no one else would think of. And I knew exactly the words I was going to illustrate on my poster: Minor and Mirror.

Okay, I know you're aware that "minor" and "mirror" are NOT homonyms, but as a fourth-grader, I was not. And, here is how I came to be so misinformed. You see, my mom would often take my siblings and me to the bar or honky-tonk where she worked. It was never for a whole shift, but maybe for a few hours until a sitter picked us up or until my mom could take us back home to be watched by my grandmother or brother. On one of these visits, I was trying to practice my reading skills, so I read the sign posted on the back wall behind the bar: NO MINORS ALLOWED!

As I read the sign aloud, the bartender gulped, looked sheepish, and quickly corrected me by saying, "Nope, that's not how it's pronounced. No MIRRORS are allowed. That word 'minor' is pronounced 'mirror.'" Well, that's all I needed to know. I now had my assignment in the bag!

I proudly went home and produced my poster with a homonym that no one else would EVER think of, using it in a sentence and even drawing the scene. Here is what I wrote in big black letters:

The MINOR saw herself in the MIRROR at Jake's Bar.

Thank God for Mrs. Fox. She didn't correct me in front of the class. She waited until after school to pull me aside and

100

explain why this wasn't a homonym. I argued with her, explaining where I had actually seen such a sign. I could tell by the look on her face that Jake's Bar was not a place I should have ever been. She didn't say this out loud; I could just tell. And if I shouldn't have been there, then neither should my mother. *That* is when I learned to be embarrassed by my mom's choice of vocations.

My mom continued to work as a barmaid for several years; I think until the early 1960s. By that time, the nightlife, the drinking, the being on her feet non-stop were all taking a toll on her health. Not that her next choice of careers was much easier.

Motel (Friendship Inn) and Theater Maid

Although barely more respectable, my mom also worked as a hotel maid at the Friendship Inn during the day. Because this was a part-time job, dependent on how booked the motel was, Mom also held the barmaid positions simultaneously. On Saturday and Sunday mornings, my mother also cleaned the local theater, which was only open on Friday and Saturday nights in the small town of Altus, Oklahoma. As an adult, when I look back at this time, I figure my mother was working a 60–80 hour week with no time off, no benefits, and no vacation.

More than a few times, I went with Mom to clean the motel rooms, but I'm sure I was in the way more than I helped. Not so with the theater—my brother and I were a lot of help—he more than I—in that we swept the auditorium while my mom cleaned the bathrooms (*Yuck* doesn't even begin to describe those!) and the concession stand.

There was some sort of blower that my brother would use, starting at the top of the theater, blowing everything down to the bottom row. I would follow behind him with a broom because things got stuck. The perk of this job was that my mom let us keep all the change we found, and it was usually a few dollars worth. Spilled popcorn is one thing, but I have never understood why people would throw down cups and popcorn containers. Trash cans were located in several places.

One other perk of this job was that my mom earned free passes to the theater for us. She rarely went—too busy working the second job at the bars—but my brother, sister, and I went as often as possible. I still love going to the movies. I hope that after COVID-19 passes, we will someday be able to return to theaters.

Even with these miserable jobs, Mom taught us valuable lessons. To this day, I ALWAYS clean up after myself and my family in a theater, or any type of public event, for that matter. I also leave hotel rooms in as clean a condition as I am able, even making my bed if I'm there for a multiple-night stay. And again, I try to educate others—always leave a $5 or $10/night tip for the hotel maid, along with a note of thanks. Many of them are in the same boat my mother was in—trying to make a living, maybe even supporting kids, with little in the way of skills.

Snack Bar Clerk at Base Pool

Once my mom married Chick, she quit the waitressing job at the NCO Club. Actually, she was required to do so because it was against the rules for a married couple to work together. Naturally, it was the woman who was expected to quit.

Financial needs, however, continued, so my mom got a job running the NCO Club Pool Snack Bar. I remember the pool being open only in the summer months of June, July, and August, seven days a week, from morning until sundown. If she worked other than those three months, I really don't remember.

Again, this was a job with perks, at least for us kids. We were allowed to swim for *free!* We also got all the snacks and Cokes we wanted, within reason. The most memorable thing I can remember about my mother holding this job was the time she talked a couple of young men into dropping a Baby Ruth candy bar into the pool. (Shades of Caddy Shack, I know!) For some reason, my mom needed to get off work early, but the Club manager refused to reassign someone to cover her shift. The candy bar trick worked; they closed early to drain the pool, her pay wasn't docked, and my mother was able to do whatever she had planned.

Although this was not the best example of work ethic for my mother to model for us kids, another lesson had been taught: where there is a will, there is a way.

Salesperson (Encyclopedia Britannica, the Great Books, Insurance, Real Estate)

During my high school years, Mom was now in her 40s. She gave up the bars, restaurants, snack bars, motels, and theaters and got the first decent job she had ever had since her short-lived career as a medical receptionist. She was hired by Encyclopedia Britannica to set up a kiosk in the Altus Air Base BX, or Base Exchange. The BX is where military personnel and their dependents can purchase goods like clothing, household items, and department store items for a reduced price with no sales tax. One has to have a military ID to shop there.

My mother was a natural-born salesperson. We used to joke that she could "sell ice cubes to an Eskimo." That truly is not an exaggeration. I was always amazed at her ability to talk someone into buying almost anything. In another time and place, she would have made a heck of a stockbroker. This job with Encyclopedia Britannica was her calling. She didn't get the job because someone knew her father or because of her youth and beauty (as those old Hollis gossips claimed). She got it because of her sales ability. For the first time in a long time, she had a job with regular daytime hours. For the first time, she had a job that wasn't demeaning or where she would be treated disrespectfully. For the first time, she had a job where people automatically thought she was well-educated; after all, she *must* have had a college degree in order to be selling encyclopedias.

Unlike many of her peers, my mother never spoke as if she were illiterate or uneducated. I do not remember her ever using poor grammar unless she was trying to make a point (e.g., "I *ain't never* gonna do *that!*"). She also had an unerring ability to match her speech to that of her customer, potential boyfriend, or whomever. If the person had only a limited vocabulary, Mom would speak plainly, using simple words but still using correct grammar. Don't misunderstand me—she never spoke down to a person. She had an innate talent to simply speak in a manner that put each person at ease. If the person had a better grasp of the English language, she would speak on their level, doing a great job of hiding any ignorance on her part. She had a decent vocabulary.

In more prosperous times, we subscribed to *Readers Digest*, and she would always do the vocabulary section, "Increase Your Word Power" vocabulary quiz. She could do math in her head, a skill I've never had. And she read copiously. I am not claiming that she read edifying tomes, but she did read. She had an uncanny gift of being able to relate to anyone, at any time, on any level. As I said, she was a natural-born salesperson ... or politician if times had been different.

The perk of this particular job was that we had an up-to-date set of Encyclopedia Britannica in our home. This helped tremendously when I was preparing for the ACT exam. The downside of this job was that my mom expected me to man the booth on weekends when I wasn't in school, to help earn my keep, and to give her some time off. Plus, my mother saw my youth as another draw for young airmen as potential buyers. She judged my success by the number of "leads" I was able to obtain. Leads were the person's name and telephone number as well as an appointment to actually sit down and sell the product. It wasn't difficult to get the leads. I wasn't butt-ugly, but even if I had been, the young and often lonely airmen were happy to get to talk to a young woman.

I cannot begin to tell you how much I hated this. I felt as if I were being pimped out. And, I felt that I was somehow cheating these young airmen; after all, how many of them *really* needed a set of encyclopedias? One young airman, named Elmer, became infatuated with me. I'm sorry to say I was not kind. I was immature and not able to properly handle the situation. I don't think I broke any hearts, but I will never be proud of the role my mother put me in so that she could get sales leads.

As with every other aspect of my mom's life, this, too, left its mark on me. I have always known I am NOT a salesperson, nor did I ever want this occupation. Don't ask me what I was thinking when, at one point in my teaching career, I decided to quit and study for the Series 7 exams to become a stockbroker for Edward Jones. I completed the training, passed all the tests, and actually opened an Edward Jones Investment office in a nearby town. My success ended there ... I found that I could not sell "a $10 bill for a buck." Yes, I did a bang-up job of teaching investing to young or new investors, but I could *not* close a sale. I got *none* of my mother's sales genes. I went back into teaching.

Over the years, the sales job at the air base evolved into selling the Great Books—yes, we got a set of those too. But as the years passed, and government cutbacks resulted in the BX being scaled back, and the air base itself all but being closed, my mom had to find other sources of revenue.

By this time, she was married to Buck, but both my sisters were in high school or college, so her expenses had also gone up. She started selling life insurance. I believe it was Mutual of Omaha for many years, but she also sold a couple of other brands. This was a job where Mom's people skills really shined. She was able to sell to the most successful of clients like doctors or lawyers, as well as to those who lived from welfare check to welfare check.

Her last sales position was as a Realtor. My mom was obviously intelligent because she passed her real estate exam with flying colors. Perhaps her eighth-grade education of yesteryear was better than some high school educations of today. She was an *excellent* realtor. Again, she was attractive, well-spoken, and knew how to make a property's good points stand out while down-playing the faults as if they did not matter.

To say that Mom taught us to always focus on the positive, to find the silver lining, would be an understatement.

Lessons I Have Learned from My Mom's Jobs

I am very proud of my mother in that we NEVER went on welfare or food stamps. Second and third jobs were the answer when times got tough. The only "hand-out" I can remember was standing in line a few times with my grandparents in the early '50s to get government cheese and powdered milk—I still can't drink that stuff.

Although the iconic country song for bad jobs is "Take This Job and Shove It" by Johnny Paycheck, I chose not to use it for the subtitle of this chapter because my mom never gave us that impression. Don't get me wrong, she had *horrible* jobs, but she was *always grateful* for employment. She demonstrated this attitude of gratitude every single day of her life, and it definitely rubbed off on us kids.

Throughout every single job my mother ever held, she always gave 100 percent, plus working when she was sick and doing what was asked of her even when it wasn't part of the job. She went above and beyond to try and get ahead, be the top salesperson, get the most tips, and to get the raise when one was possible. She had a work ethic before that term even existed. To put it as she did, "always give more than a day's work for a day's pay."

Not only I, but my siblings followed in her footsteps in terms of her work ethic, if not her career choices. My brother never missed a day's work in the 30-plus years he worked for the phone company. He refused to join the union because he knew he would never go on strike. My sister also had perfect attendance in her job, even when she was battling stage 4 cancer.

I can't claim to have had perfect attendance in my teaching career, but close to it. I very rarely used my sick leave for actual sickness but instead used days for professional development or taking kids to compete in various state and national business competitions.

In our respective careers, all three of us were quick to volunteer for extra duties, even if it didn't mean extra pay. We were also competitive to try and do a better job than what was expected. We all consistently took classes to improve ourselves and our knowledge.

If you caught my use of "three of us" instead of "four of us," that will be explained in Chapters 6 and 9. Regretfully, my mom's work ethos was worn thin by the time she was raising my youngest sister.

For myself, as a teacher, I considered anything less than an absolutely perfect evaluation to be a failure. This included my evaluations from my superiors and those from my students. I was not an easy teacher, but I like to think I was a fair one. I taught business and computers for almost 30 years at high school and college levels, so I believed in my subject matter. I was teaching my students skills they could use whether or not they went to college.

I was determined my students would have a way to make a living, no matter what life threw at them—divorce, death of a spouse, kids, or even health issues. When I taught an administrative assistant program at the junior college level, I was passionate about helping the women in my courses—it was rare to have a man enrolled—to be as employable as possible, with skills that would enable them to find decent, respectable jobs. I absolutely know my upbringing and the struggles I witnessed with my own mother were the driving force behind my passion. If there were one idea that I consistently tried to imprint upon my students, it was "pull yourself up by your bootstraps." My mother had always demonstrated to us, "never let your background define you."

We also learned that working long and hard does not always equate to lots of money. Mom's sporadic income over the years drilled that lesson home. She did her best to provide well for each of us, but sometimes her decisions backfired or caused great embarrassment for one of us kids.

One such time occurred in my grade school years when I wore a lovely dress to school. It was new to me, but it wasn't new. My mom had bought a number of outfits from a friend who had a daughter the same age as I, but "they were last year's clothes." The concept of having new clothes each school year was quite foreign to us at that time; clothes were replaced only when outgrown or ruined.

So off I skipped to school, thinking I was really something. In the third grade, I was the reigning Jacks champion at recess. This didn't sit well with Marita, the girl whose dress I had on. She announced to her circle of friends, "See that dress Dorenda has on? I threw it away last year, but I guess she dug it out of the trash."

I was devastated. I didn't even go back inside when recess ended. I simply walked home from the playground and told my mom I would never wear any of those "stupid outfits" again. Mom may have called the school to say I was ill; I don't know. For the longest time, I was angry at my mother for making me wear someone else's hand-me-downs. In my immaturity, I couldn't see that she was trying her best to put me in nice clothing, despite her lack of funds. She didn't realize how cruel and mean some kids are.

On my birthday, when I turned 12, my mom and her husband du jour, Chick McGee, announced, "*Now*, you're 12, *now* you're an adult, and *now*, you need to start acting like one. You need to help out around here. You need to find a job."

Obviously, they didn't mean I had to quit school, but I realized I needed to seek opportunities to make money. My older brother, Rodney, was a prime example—he literally started working odd jobs when he was 8 years old. So, over the next five years, I did anything I could to make extra money; handouts, such as an allowance, were over. I babysat, of course; I can't imagine any parent leaving their kids with a 12-year-old, but it happened. I also cleaned dog poop out of yards. Yes, I was learning amazing vocational skills.

At the age of 13, I was employed at the local donut shop, which opened at 5 a.m. I didn't have to "trudge five miles in the snow," but I definitely had to walk the ten or so blocks from our house on C Street down to North Main at 4:30 a.m. every day in the summer and every weekend for about a year. I specifically remember being paid $1.15 per hour because that was my first real paycheck with taxes and everything. The minimum wage was $1.60 in 1968, so I guess I was paid as a restaurant worker, even though there were no tips. I didn't have a checking account, thus the paycheck was handed to my mom, and she gave me money as she saw fit.

The most vivid memory I have from this job is of one cold and frosty morning when a woman came in with her three kids, none older than 10, at most. We had barely opened, and it was still dark outside. The shop owner had finished the last batch of donuts and had left for the day. It was like one of those heart-wrenching movies—the little kids were glued to the display windows, eyes big and round, looking at all the donuts and pastries. None of them were well dressed and certainly not properly dressed for the cold weather. Even if the mother hadn't been asking the price of each item, I quickly assessed that they were short of funds and probably traveling. North Main was actually Highway 283, a major route heading north and south through the state. I have no solid facts to suspect that the woman was running from something or someone, but I definitely had "the feeling."

If you have ever been in a bakery-type store, you have probably noticed a shelf where "day-old" items are placed, usually at half-price. We had such a display at this shop, mostly holding plain glazed donuts that had not sold the day before. It did *not* hold any of the delicious chocolate-covered crullers or cinnamon twists or jelly-filled rolls that filled the air with mouth-watering scents. (I am making myself hungry as I dredge up this memory.) Those items sold out early most every day. Of course, these very items were the ones the kids were drooling over. The disappointment on their little faces was heart-breaking when the mother told them to pick something from the day-old display.

Okay, I am about to disclose a decades-old secret. I can only hope the donut shop owner has long passed away, or he may press charges. Here is what I did. "Oh my!" I said. "*All* these donuts in this row are day-old too! I haven't transferred them over to the other shelf! Good thing my boss isn't here, or he'd be chewing me out!"

So, the lady and her three very happy kids tumbled out of the donut shop with exactly what they wanted that morning to continue their journey. I pray they reached safety. If the mother doubted my story, she didn't say anything, but I could tell she was immensely grateful.

I've thought of that incident many times over the years, and there is only one thing I would change—I would have paid the full price for the donuts out of my own pocket once the family had left. But at the age of 13, and with no money in my pocket, doing this deed in an honest way didn't occur to me.

When I was 14 or 15, I was old enough to work at the Base Exchange Watch Repair Shop. It was a little cubbyhole located in the same block as the BX. I was reliable enough that the manager gave me a key and let me open and close up shop each day I worked. I really liked this job. In addition to labeling broken watches with the owner's information so they could be repaired by an expert, I learned how to do minor jewelry repair and name tag engraving. My next job at age 16 was working the encyclopedia booth in the BX, and I've already detailed how much I detested that job.

I graduated at age 17 and knew I would do whatever it took to go to college because *that* would be my ticket out of poverty and out of my mother's house. Luckily we had a two-year college in Altus, within walking distance of our home on Sycamore. I had no car, so walking was the only option.

I had heard from others of this job called "work-study," where the college would hire you to work in various positions while you took classes. It was a God-send for me.

I had had the forethought to complete an "advanced degree" in high school, also known as "college-bound." It required that I have at least two years of foreign language, advanced math and science courses, and four years of English. I had also taken two years of typing—at one time, I could type 80 wpm—and a year of shorthand, basically so I would have the skills to earn a living in case college didn't pan out.

Oklahoma, at the time, was on an eight-point grading scale, meaning that one had to have at least a 93 for an A, a minimum of 85 for a B, and anything below 70 was failing. I was a mostly A student and had even scored high enough on the ACT exam that I received a full-paid scholarship offer from a major university (*more on that in Chapter 6*). Because of my grades and secretarial skills, I was placed in the registrar's office as my work-study assignment.

Working at the junior college was another job I *loved*. Mrs. LaVeta Vineyard, the college registrar, was my supervisor, and I truly loved that woman. She was professionalism and kindness itself, and taught me to triple-check everything I did when it came to college transcripts. She trusted me and my integrity, and I would have died before I'd ever disappoint her. For the first time, I was earning a paycheck that wasn't given to my mother first. For the first time, I was being judged on my own merits, not as the daughter of a barmaid. For the first time, I had more responsibility and respect than my peers did—Mrs. Vineyard didn't trust any of the other work-study students to handle transcripts, only me.

Altus Junior College was a breeze for me, but I didn't finish my two-year degree. I got married the second semester of my sophomore year and moved to Lawton, Oklahoma, where I completed my four-year degree at Cameron University. I never looked back, not at Altus, not at my mom's home, not at any of it. I still have never returned for a high school reunion. Thanks to Facebook, I now have some contact with old classmates, but honestly, those years were not my happiest. I prefer to live in the present.

I had two other jobs in my pre-adult life prior to marriage and college. One was in a fast food joint, which lasted one day, and the other was in a lingerie factory, Kellwood, which lasted one week. Lots of lessons were learned from both of these short-lived jobs, but nothing relevant to this book.

My mom's work ethic had a definite impact on my own career and professional choices, but also on that of my brother and sister. Both finished two-year degrees and had long careers in the telecommunications industry. My brother seems to have worked his whole life, even when he was a kid, and only retired in the last couple of years, well into his 70s. My sister started working once she was out of college and had only a short respite during the COVID-19 layoffs; she is once again working full-time, at least until she qualifies for social security.

From our mother, we all learned these things about our jobs and careers:

- Always give *more* than 100 percent.

- To goof off or give less is exactly like stealing.

- Be grateful for a job, even when it isn't your dream.

- Improve yourself—it doesn't have to be a degree or another class; reading and volunteering for extra jobs will do it.

- Be watchful for the next opportunity, but don't burn any bridges.

- Be kind and generous to others; not everyone is as fortunate as we are.

- There are no demeaning jobs, but there are people out there who will judge and treat you in a demeaning manner if you allow it; don't allow it!

I hope this chapter has made you feel good about your own job or career, maybe bringing forth memories about your own parents or family members. Perhaps it has made you think about sacrifices your parents made, or you have made in order to support the family. If so, take the time to send a note of thanks. I absolutely know that, if I had the chance, I would tell my mother how grateful I am for all she did to feed and shelter our family. As a kid, one doesn't see sacrifices or recognize when parents give up dreams. This especially hit home for me when I started my research for the next chapter.

Chapter 5

Highs and Lows

"You Looked the Other Way" by Jo Stout

You may have noticed the subtitle of this chapter and Chapter 1 of this book have my mom's name as the artist. Both are song titles of actual songs that my mother wrote and had recorded by professional singers. Younger readers may not understand what I mean when I say I have three of her records; I am talking about actual round vinyl disks played on turntables. On one of the three records, there is a fourth song on the reverse side of the LP—another word for a record, meaning long play.

The Highs

My mom was a very gifted song and jingle writer. The physical records I have are tangible proof that a person can have all the talent in the world, but talent alone will not make one successful. And, sometimes, dreams are dashed or put aside because of other pressing matters.

The first time my siblings or I became aware that our mother had this talent was in Ft. Meade, Maryland. The base was promoting safety and held a jingle contest. My mom entered the following:

"Don't stick your elbow out too far;
It might go home in another car!"

Her jingle was the winning entry! I think she was paid a whole $15. Yet, it wasn't the money that put my mom on top of the world. It was the recognition that she was more than merely a housewife, that she had talent, that she had something to offer the world. We heard the jingle all the time on the car radio, at least for a full year. Whenever we did hear it, we would all hang out the windows of our sedan and sing the jingle at the top of our lungs. (There were no seatbelt laws until the 1980s or 1990s, depending on the state.)

This experience gave my mother enough confidence to enter other jingle contests over the next few years. Some she won, some not. Usually, the prizes were products rather than cash awards. Hindsight makes me wish I had kept a record of all the rhymes and verses she created or a list of all the prizes she garnered over those years. For some reason, she stopped entering jingle competitions after we moved away from Maryland. Perhaps it was because there were no opportunities like that in small-town Oklahoma.

I have a very vivid memory of my mom, my sister, Jo, and me traveling by bus to Baltimore one day. We packed our lunches in brown paper bags. The reason we were going to the big city of Baltimore was so my mother could have one of her songs recorded by professionals. This would have been 1959 or 1960 because I wasn't enrolled in school yet.

Figure 56 Sadie Jo Stout in a Baltimore recording studio.

Once we relocated to Oklahoma, my mother's writing talents were turned to songs. She had no musical training, had never been taught any instruments or how to read music. I don't know if things might have turned out differently if she had had these talents as well as the ability to write.

My mom used her songwriting as a release; it was cheap self-therapy whenever life became too unbearable. Sometimes I would wake up in the early morning hours, shortly after my mother had come in from her barmaid shift. She would be quietly sitting at the kitchen table, writing a verse. When she spotted me, I'd get a hug and kiss, sometimes a glass of milk, and then she'd shoo me off to bed. I would stall with, "When are you coming to bed, Mommy?"

"Soon, soon. Just have to write this down while I'm thinking about it," would be her reply.

These song lyrics were sporadic, written on scraps of paper here and there, sometimes on the back of an envelope or a bill that had come in the mail. My mother was not an organized person, or at least she wasn't once we returned to live in Oklahoma. When we found the records amongst her things after she passed, I was surprised.

One of the records was recorded in Nashville, Tennessee, by Globe Recording Studio. This studio still exists. The singer hired for the demo was Mary Kaye, who, turns out, was quite a prolific singer even though I had never heard of her. The reason for the demo was that it was part of a deal my mother was trying to do with the legendary Patsy Cline. We were told at the time that my mom's song, "You Looked the Other Way," was being considered by Ms. Cline for inclusion on her next album. I remember the phone call from Ms. Cline's agent and how ecstatic my mother was. She was absolutely beside herself and made me promise on her life—remember, I'm the one who can't keep secrets—not to mention anything to my dad. For once, I kept my mouth shut. I didn't understand the secrecy at the time, but I think I do now. My mom saw her dreams coming true, financially enabling her to leave my dad and choose her own path.

Fate had other plans for my mom, however, because Patsy Cline died in a horrific airplane crash in 1963, within weeks of that phone call to my mother. A dark cloud landed on my mom when we heard the news of Cline's death that night, and at the time, I didn't think Mom would ever come out from under it.

I was very wrong. This one incident made me realize how resilient and optimistic my mother was. She did NOT allow it to destroy her dreams even though nothing more ever came of her songs—no more record deals, no more phone calls from agents, no more demos being recorded. In spite of this, she remained confident throughout her life that her ship was coming in; she never gave up hope. She was known to say things like, *"when* I win the lottery," or *"when* I sell this song," never "If."

It was this buoyant, expectant attitude that made my mother who she was—always positive that success and wealth were barely over the horizon. I would hear her friends or co-workers say, "Aww, Jo, that ship has sailed." But Mom would reply, a smile on her face, "Not without me, it hasn't!"

I *loved* this aspect of my mom's personality, even though I refuted it when I became a sarcastic teenager. I really don't know how my mother could stand me as I look back at my ugly attitude. But, Mom wouldn't let reality or my downer viewpoint stop her in her tracks. She would always bounce back from each and every setback, and believe me, there were plenty.

It had to have been this positive defiance in the face of despair that caused my mom to keep marrying. She never gave up hope that the next one would be the right one. She believed with all her heart and soul that true love was just one marriage away.

My youngest sister, Taffy, inherited my mom's always hopeful attitude. To this day, in spite of all the horrible things that have happened to her *(more in Chapter 9)*, she sounds exactly like Mom in expressing her rosy outlook. Even my sister, Jo, has a dose of Mom's optimism; I've always said that if Mary Poppins came to life, she would be my sister, Jo. Me? I *try* to have a positive attitude at all times, and for the most part, I succeed. If you measured mine on a scale of 1 to 10, with Mom being a 10+, I might be a 6 or 7 on my best days.

Mom's other best talent was her ability to sell—anything to anybody. I never appreciated this skill as I was growing up. Shame on me because it was this ability that put a roof over our heads and food in our bellies. Truth be told, I thought I was better than she was because I would never stretch the truth ("You'll use these encyclopedias every day of your life, and it'll really impress all the girls.") or tell lies of omission. ("This house has great bones" *even though all the electrical wiring is shot.*)

No, it wasn't until I spent two years of my life preparing to be an investment broker that I realized I *really* needed my mom's sales talent. I had none, zip, zero, nada.

However, I evidently *did* get a good dose of my mother's positive outlook because the training I received to become a broker has enabled me to secure my own future, and it helped me be a better business teacher.

My mother became more community-minded as she aged. She was a member of the Red Hats Society of Altus, and regularly attended their luncheons and fundraisers. I once made the mistake of referring to the Red Hats as "a bunch of old gossiping biddies." Mom immediately set me straight in no uncertain terms. Yes, they met for breakfasts or luncheons, but they always had a purpose, whether it was providing a scholarship for a deserving student to attend Western Oklahoma State College (formerly Altus

Junior College) or to provide a holiday meal for needy families.

Figure 57 Mom was a member of the local Red Hat Society.

She also served as an Altus Chamber of Commerce Ambassador, assisting with new business openings and serving as a mentor to women-owned businesses. She was very proud of this role. Plus, it gave her an excuse to wear one of her always-present business suits.

Ribbon cutting

Chamber of Commerce ambassadors held a ribbon cutting for Universal House of Beauty, 116 S. Main, recently. From left are Trisha Westfall, Mike Trachman, Forrest Cox, Beverly Creed, Janice Bohann, Joe Buchanan, Casandra Allen, Donella Christian, Mary Willis, Jimmy Young, Renee West, Pam Willis, John Horschler, Gary Larson and Jesse Turner. The child standing behind the ribbon is J.C. Chavarra.

Figure 58 Mom, 5th from left, Altus Chamber of Commerce Ambassador.

"Jo is the luckiest person I know" was a phrase we would often hear from Mom's casual acquaintances as we were growing up. This observation was obviously *not* based on Mom's husband choices, but rather on her ability to win drawings and contests. Whether it was popping a balloon to find a prize, a name drawn out of a box, or picking the right square, Mom was indeed lucky. None of these prizes amounted to much, but they continued to fuel Mom's confidence that the "big prize" was right around the corner.

Big money winner

Safeway manager Carroll Thacker, right, presents Jo Buchanan with a check for $1,000 for winning the store's game.

Figure 59 Mom featured in the Altus Times.

I already told you, that Mom was a people person, able to get along or talk with anyone from any walk of life. So, I don't know if Mom's other superpower is an offshoot talent related to being a people person, but she had an uncanny knack for putting the right people together. You might think I am talking about match-making, and to an extent, I am. But I am also talking about friendships and even adoptions.

Throughout her working life, people would come to Mom, saying things like, "Jo, you introduced so and so to each other, and they're happy as larks. Can't you find someone for me?" Mom would smile, reach for her coffee, and an otherworldly, thoughtful expression would come over her face. Sometimes, she would respond immediately with, "I know exactly the person for you!" Sometimes, she would try to instill a little hope by saying, "Let me think about it a while. There's the right someone out there for *all* of us."

I have no data on which to base this claim, but the matches she made did all seem to work out. This gave her pleasure and created lifelong friends. At her memorial, two different couples came up to me and told me, "If it hadn't been for Jo, we never would have met!"

She was able to match people to jobs, people to friendships, even people to animals. But the most amazing story my brother and I heard regarding her ability to put people together happened after her death. We were visiting the church where her memorial would be held. One of the staff there pulled us aside and shared the following story with us:

"Jo is the reason we now have grandchildren. Back in the day, we couldn't have children of our own, and adoption was too expensive. Jo had sold us a life insurance policy, so she knew of our struggles to create a family. About the same time, she also had a very young client that had recently given birth to a baby boy, but the baby was not being well cared for, for various reasons—finances, youth maybe, no husband, we don't know. At any rate, the young mother told Jo that she needed to give the baby up so he could have a better life. Your mom immediately contacted us, and we were able to adopt our son. She even set us up with one of her lawyer friends, so the adoption was affordable. Now our son has two kids of his own, our grandchildren. None of this would have happened without Jo. She was our angel."

I have to tell you, that if *this* were the only thing I had ever heard about my mother, I would think this alone paved her way into heaven. My brother and I were speechless. Never once did my mom tell us about this or brag about it. Seems my sister, Jo, has another trait from my mother—the ability to keep a secret.

The Lows

I've read somewhere that some personalities can't handle the stresses that come with being gifted or talented, so as strange as this sounds, they sabotage themselves, they self-destruct. Our media is filled with these kinds of stories, usually about movie stars (Marilyn Monroe), rock stars (Janis Joplin), even business prodigies (Kate Spade). Perhaps my mother fell into this category because, most certainly, a number of her problems and low points in her life were the result of poor decisions and even poorer behavior.

But as I look at the subtitle for this chapter, I'm also inclined to think that "'Fate' Looked the Other Way." We all have heard the cliché, "They were just born under an unlucky star." There is actually some scientific data to suggest this cliché might have some truth to it rather than simply superstition. According to a January 24th, 2007 article in *New Scientist Magazine,* "Born Under a Bad Sign?" details that the time of year one is born affects one's personality, health, and chances of developing a mental illness.[1] "For people born in the northern hemisphere in February, March, and April, the risk of developing schizophrenia is between 5 and 10 percent greater than for those born at other times of the year."

Not saying my mother was schizophrenic or had mental illness, but I do believe that the historical period of time when she was born, and where she was born, both have a

---

[1] Alison Motluk, "Born under A Bad Sign?," *New Scientist* (New Scientist, January 24, 2007), https://www.newscientist.com/article/mg19325881-700-born-under-a-bad-sign.

bearing on her "lack of luck." As I've already addressed, the world events taking place molded part of her personality. Her disposition, although optimistic, was one where she was always seeking the greener pastures, the "grass is greener on the other side of the fence," so to speak.

Poor Decision #1: Booze

When life disappointed her, my mother turned to alcohol. She did not drink hard liquor—that was too expensive. But she could put away a six-pack or two of Coors beer without blinking an eye. I don't know when my mother started drinking. Maybe she did so as a barmaid. How many of her customers offered to buy another drink if she would have one with them? After all, she was a pretty woman. And, I'm going to make a biased guess here that most of these men were in a honky-tonk or bar because they were lonely, to begin with. More drinks sold meant a larger tip. I can reason out how this might have happened.

But maybe it had nothing to do with her barmaid stint and everything to do with her failed marriages and/or failed careers. Perhaps, all these disappointments eventually took their toll, and she had to find something to "dull the pain," at least for that evening.

I've referred to my mother as a "highly functioning alcoholic," meaning she could be drinking or even drunk, but the average person would not have known it. When drinking, Mom did not slur her words, she didn't stumble, and she didn't get all maudlin. She *did* get mean (*but more on that in Chapter 6)*; she was not a loveable drunk for sure.

I don't recall my mother ever drinking more than a beer or two during the day, usually with a meal, especially with pizza. No, her drinking occurred at night, usually after a work shift, sometimes on a night off. I can also swear that Mom never lost a day of work to a hangover or being drunk. She "functioned" with her alcohol addiction as well as could be expected, never missing work, never losing a job. She never saw her drinking as a problem. As Dr. Phil says, "You can't change what you don't acknowledge."

I refer to Mom's drinking as an addiction because it was. She *had* to have her Coors every night. Supposedly we are of Native American heritage, and if this is true, it is also true that this ethnic group has a predisposition to alcoholism because of a difference in the way they metabolize alcohol (according to the National Institute of Health).[2] Susceptibility to addictions may literally be in our genes.

To say that my mother's drinking affected me would be an understatement. I never took my first drink of alcohol until I was in my 40s, and I have *never* been drunk, ever in my life. I hated the loss of control my mother had when she was drinking, and I absolutely never wanted to experience that for myself. My sister, Jo, was affected even more deeply—she's never had a single drop of alcohol touch her lips. Both of us chose spouses that do not drink. Regretfully, my brother, Rodney, had a period of time in his life when drinking and getting drunk were the norm. Thank God he found the Lord in his early adulthood and has never had a drop since. It is obvious to all of us that we cannot handle alcohol, so it's best to avoid it.

---

[2] "In This Issue," National Institute on Alcohol Abuse and Alcoholism (U.S. Department of Health and Human Services), accessed February 17, 2022, https://pubs.niaaa.nih.gov/publications/arh301/3-4.htm.

Poor Decision #2: Looking for Love in All the Wrong Places

The reasons most of my mother's marriages failed can be attributed to one or more of these categories: cheating/adultery, drinking, abuse, finances, and absences. I have always been an analytical person, even as a child. So it was natural for me to dissect these failed relationships, find the causes, and thus attempt to avoid said disasters in my own life.

Therefore, it is unfathomable for me to understand why my mother continued to find her "next husband" in places like bars, honky-tonks, or military bases. It was perfectly logical to me that if you find someone in a bar or honky-tonk, it is quite likely they will have a tendency to drink too much. And drinking too much often leads to cheating or adultery or abuse, or all three.

I'm not sure I am correct in putting cheating and adultery into two different categories, but I have always thought of it this way:

Cheating is when one flirts with, pays attention to, or perhaps even has minor physical contact—kissing, hugging, or dancing—with a partner who is in a committed relationship with another person, especially when the other person is not present or would not approve. Few adults, myself included, are totally innocent of these "harmless flirtations."

Adultery is physically consummating that flirtatious relationship. In my opinion, cheating oftentimes leads to adultery. I mean, *People*! The very word, *cheating*, means doing something you shouldn't.

As for the abuse being a result of drinking, I would agree that some abusers need not be drinking to have an excuse to beat on a spouse, child, or animal. Again, from my own experience, I am merely indicating that drinking often led to abusive behavior on the part of my mother and some of her husbands. The targets were either my brother, myself, and sometimes, my mother. Yet again, another reason I very rarely drink. It is also why I choose to avoid certain friends or acquaintances if I know that alcohol will be part of the event.

So what about the military posts and bases? I think initially, my mom thought a spouse in the military would mean escaping the small towns of Hollis and Altus. However, when times got tough, she always returned to one of these two towns. Sometimes the greener grass isn't so green when you get there.

I think she also thought life in the military would mean "benefits" such as medical care, cheaper groceries, housing, etc. Turns out, that medical care, grocery selection, and housing weren't always up to par with the civilian options.

She also perhaps thought a regular paycheck from the military would be like manna from heaven as compared to the sporadic income of farming. Too bad she didn't have the internet back then so she could look up the wages of the young airmen and navy specialists. It was not even above poverty level. Understandable why she raised her standards to sergeants or lieutenants in subsequent marriages.

Even if she had chosen a colonel, the results would probably have been the same because my mom was completely untrusting of absences. She imagined the worst every time one of her husbands was deployed: "He's cheating on me, I just know it!"

She actually wasn't wrong in the case of my father, Joe. He did, in fact, set up house with a woman in Germany, Heidi, who subsequently married my father once my mom divorced him the second time. My half-sister, Angelika, whom I mentioned in Chapter 2, was the result of my dad's relationship with Heidi. She was born after me but before my sister, Jo.

Whether she unjustly accused any of her other spouses, I don't know. But it wasn't only the suspicion that made absences unacceptable to my mother. She could not tolerate a relationship where the other person was gone a good deal of the time, whether it was deployments or second jobs.

As I've aged, I realize there are many people who are like this, both men and women. These people, as was my own mother, are dependent on their spouse's presence every day or night. Sometimes, the two don't even speak, but it's unbearable to be separated. I've heard the term "joined at the hip" to describe this. I personally think it is a control issue, or maybe a trust issue on the part of one or both spouses. So, if one has this personality trait, choosing a spouse in the military or one who travels for a living is absolutely ludicrous, in my opinion. Please understand that I recognize there are those rare couples out there who are truly devoted to one another, and it makes both upset to be separated. I am just saying none of my mother's unions fell into this category.

Poor Decision #3: Liar, Liar, Pants on Fire!

I've already cataloged many of the ways my mom prevaricated. I've always liked that word better than the word *lying*—it sounds so much more acceptable. To prevaricate implies one is misleading, but not downright *lying*! If I prevaricate, I am meandering around the truth, not purposely *lying* to you! After all, I would never be *lying* to anyone; I'd simply be telling less than the whole truth!

Okay, okay, enough of my pulling your leg. The above paragraph sort of demonstrates how my mom operated regarding facts and truth. She and Bill Clinton would have talked circles around each other.

As my grandmother said more times than I can count, "Sadie Jo lies when the truth is easier." And, yes, she did. Most of the time, we think people lie in order to avoid punishment, or perhaps to get something they don't deserve or to hide something from someone.

In my mother's case, all of these could have been reasons, but I also think she lied to see if she could "get one over on you." Perhaps she was judging, "just how gullible and trusting is this person?" Perhaps she was testing to see how much a person trusted her. As her child, I learned to verify most everything she ever said if it were important enough to me. Some things weren't worth the effort. In today's world of instant fact-checking on the internet (like we can always trust *that* source), my mom would have been hard-pressed to tell some of her whoppers. But usually, it wasn't tall tales she told. It was simply day-to-day facts.

What it all boils down to is this: I believe my mom lied because *that* was the world she wanted to believe in, the world she pretended existed, the world she would have chosen if she could control things. You see, she was lying to the *one* person with whom she should have always been truthful ... herself. The rest of us were collateral damage.

I'm sure that my mother's lies hurt me as I was growing up, but I cannot think of a single one now. However, it was a lie she told to my own 4-year-old son that hurt me to the core. My mother had come to Lawton, Oklahoma, where I lived with my husband and son, to take care of something for her insurance business. When she called to tell me she was coming, I offered to take her to lunch so we could see each other, and she could see my son, Derrick. Toward the end of the meal, my mother saw a circus poster that would be in town the next week. My mom told my son she would be back to take him to the circus. She made a big deal out of saying what all they would see, what she would buy him, and all the fun they would have. She promised him. It took every ounce of restraint I had to keep from interrupting and scolding her for making promises she would not keep.

Needless to say, Derrick was beside himself with excitement and questions: "When will she be back? How many days will that be? Can we go sooner?" I was more and more stricken with his every question and every bounce up and down.

I waited until my mom got into her car, and we got into ours. As I buckled my son in, I tried to explain, "Derrick, Grandma means what she says; she *really* does want to take you to the circus. *But*, she won't be able to because she has lots of other things she has to do." His plaintive, "But she promised!" was counteracted with my own pledge to take him myself. "And, if we see Grandma there, you two can sit together." He had the resilience of a 4-year-old because it didn't seem to faze him when my mother never showed up

136

on the day of the performance. He was perfectly content to be going with his mom and dad.

Lessons I have learned from the highs and lows of Mom's life:

- Life isn't always fair. Whew! How many times have we heard *that* one!?

- *Never* give up on your talents or gifts. Even if you can't make a living with it/them, let your talents shine as a hobby or in a volunteer setting.

- Always stay positive, hope for the best—and when the best doesn't come easily, then work harder to make it a reality.

- Even the worst person you can think of probably has some redeeming quality that you can't easily see, so next time you judge someone as unworthy, try to see them in the Maker's eyes.

- Do everything in moderation, whether it be drinking *or* marrying. ☺

- Be conscientious of telling the truth, the whole truth, and nothing but the truth. Lies of omission are still lies. To paraphrase Shakespeare, a lie by any other name is still a lie.

Lastly, for this chapter of highs and lows, I would like to share with you the "Four-Way Test" as adopted by the Rotary Club International in 1943 and still used today in 220 countries:[3]

---

[3] "4-Way Test," Rotary Club of Houston, TX, accessed February 17, 2022, https://www.rotaryhouston.org/Stories/4-way-test.

"Of all the things we think, say, or do, ask the following four questions:

- Is it the truth?

- Is it fair to all concerned?

- Will it build goodwill and better friendships?

- Will it be beneficial to all concerned?

And in 2015, this fifth question was added:

- Is it fun?"

If we could all monitor our actions and statements with these five tenets, I believe the world would be a better place.

I also believe that every being ever created on this earth was gifted with a talent. Each of us should try our best to find that talent and use it to make the world a better place. Have you recognized your talent? Did you inherit it from a family member? And one last burning question as I take you into the next chapter: Why were ELBOWS the all-consuming safety issue in the 1960s instead of seatbelts!?

Okay, it's time to share my mother's parenting skills, or lack thereof, with the rest of the world in this next chapter. Spoiler alert: I turned out okay, so don't worry, it's not that bad.

Chapter 6

Parenting 101

"Wild One" by Faith Hill

In spite of our childhood of upheaval, my siblings and I loved our mother with all our hearts. Nevertheless, we were not angels. I was a world-class smart-aleck, and my brother didn't always hang with the best of kids. My youngest sister, Taffy, was hell on wheels. Literally, she crashed the family car after stealing it at age 13. My sister, Jo, was the only one among us who always seemed to do as she was told; she took after my grandmother in her demeanor—calm, quiet, and thoughtful in her actions.

It pains me to say that the bad behavior of all of us combined (or at least me, Rodney, and Jo; we will leave Taffy out of the equation for it totally skews the point I am making here) paled in comparison to my mother's antics. Don't misunderstand me; she was NOT a bad person. Immature? Yes. Inattentive? Yes. Misguided? Yes.

Some of her behaviors don't make sense to me, even in hindsight. I'm sure her immaturity resulted from being spoiled and catered to by parents who were too old to fight her. But, her unfortunate decisions, disastrous judgment, and dreadful priorities ... perhaps those resulted from living a disappointing life.

My grandmother was the best mother in the world, from not only my viewpoint, but that of my aunts and uncles. So with Grandma as a role model, how could my mom have been such a poor parent?

I'm going to stop myself right there because a truly poor parent is one that never puts the children first, doesn't care about whether or not they are clothed, fed, or housed properly. *That* was *not* my mother! She was a *good* provider. We were *always* clothed, fed, and housed; none of us were ever given up for adoption—certainly the easier, and many times, best choice for most single moms.

My calling her a "poor parent" has everything to do with those aspects of her personality that I wished had been different. Wishes are like fishes that were never caught. However, here is my Wish List:

I wish she had thought before she spoke.

I wish she had not cussed.

I wish there had been more peace and less turmoil or violence in the house.

I wish she had not married so many men because I hated that my siblings and I had different last names.

I wish she hadn't been so inattentive and self-absorbed.

I wish she hadn't been so controlling.

I wish she had had a stronger moral compass.

I wish she had been a better role model in terms of character, not only as a provider.

Before I start detailing all my mom's "sins," let me share a quote I saw the other day on Pinterest: "Counting other people's sins does not make you a saint." I absolutely *know*

I am not. I sure hope no one decides to write a book about me and all *my* faults!

Watch What You Say; Say What You Mean

Let's start with one of my earliest memories—probably one of my worst memories.

I was 3 years old. My mother was in a Hollis grocery store and had my new baby sister, Jo, in the cart. I don't remember if Rodney was with us or not. My mom, exasperated and tired of my wandering away from the cart, said, "If you don't stay right here, I'm going to leave you!"

Being a small town, the grocery store was Gossip Central, so my mom was constantly stopping to talk to each and every person, and to show off my new sister. Who knows what was going through my pointed little head? Perhaps I was jealous, probably bored, and easily distracted. Of course, I wandered off.

I have no concept of how much time passed, but before long, I realized my mom was not in the same aisle she had been, and I started panicking. Then I remembered what she had said, so I headed out the front door of the store; surely I could catch her before she actually drove off!

Instead of seeing my mother, I saw an old man leaning against the building; I thought I had seen him before, perhaps with my grandfather. He recognized me, and I trustingly put my hand in his when he told me he would take me to my mom. He did not.

I have no memory of the car ride or arriving at my grandparents' home; I have no memory of anything except being on the back porch of their house. The man kept trying

143

to get me to sit on his lap, but I was too busy running around, chasing chickens, as I recall. The worst thing I recollect is that the man, sitting in a rickety chair on that back porch, exposed himself to me; if anything else occurred, my mind has blocked it out, and for that, I am most grateful.

Again, no concept of time, but I heard a siren and yelling from the front of my grandparents' home. It was my mom in a police car. I was screaming, "Mommy! Mommy!" when she came tearing around the side of the house. She was crying and hugging me, but at the same time, yelling, "Don't you *ever* do that to me again! *What* is *wrong* with you!? You scared me to death!"

I realized then that I was in *big* trouble. It was all my fault, and now I was really going to get it. The policeman took the man to the police car, then came back and started asking me questions. Looking back, I realize they were trying to ascertain if I had been molested. My mother kept saying, "She's fine, no harm, he's a friend of my daddy."

Knowing I was already in trouble for wandering off, and thinking it was all my doing, especially with my mother saying the man was a friend, I shut down. I did *not* mention the exposure or anything else. I kept saying, "I want my mommy. I want my mommy."

Over the next days or weeks, who knows, I caught snippets of conversations between my mom, my grandpa and grandma, and even my Uncle Dewey. Things like: "She will be fine," "Best not to let anyone know about this," "She won't remember anything," "I'll take care of him," and "no need to get the police involved." In my child's mind, I thought they were trying to keep *me* from going to jail for having

144

wandered off and getting Grandpa's friend in trouble. I promise, my behavior was exemplary for the next several weeks.

My grandfather, maybe even my uncle, did indeed "take care of him," for the man supposedly left town, skipping bail, and was never heard from again. I later learned he was a known pedophile, and he was *not* a friend of my grandfather, merely a customer of his produce.

My mother had lied to the police officer, thinking she was protecting me, keeping me from being in the spotlight. Of course, the man meant me harm … any sane person would have taken me back into the grocery store to look for my mother or called the police. At the very least, he would have sat on the front porch with me, not hidden in the back of the house.

As a young adult, there was a time when I was angry at my mother for not having pursued legal justice on this man by taking me to the hospital for an exam or letting the police officer question me. Perhaps, though, my mom did the right thing in shoving this incident under the carpet. By never giving it more attention, not allowing anyone to dwell on it, or pity me, I grew up fine with no stigmas of having "been molested." And, my grandfather was my first hero.

From this incident, I learned to never say something to a child that you don't mean to carry out. My mom showed her immaturity by saying what she did. I overhear parents say similar things every day of my life … walk down any aisle in Walmart. Kids will take what you say at face value; they are very literal. But, eventually, they will realize everything you say is a bluff, and then they will stop listening to anything you say.

To "only say what I mean" has served me very well, both in my career as a teacher and my personal life as a spouse and mother. Now, as I am fulfilling my role as a grandparent, I realize how important this lesson is. Watch your words.

Fussing and Cussing

The last sentence of the above paragraph could be repeated here: Watch your words. This includes cussing and fussing. My first husband had an aunt and uncle by marriage whom I dreaded to visit. It wasn't because I didn't like the two of them; it was because they never stopped fussing at one another during our visit; I can only assume it went on all the time. "Joyce, you never have a GOL-DARNED (*word changed to protect the innocent*) place to sit in the place; your junk is in every chair!" It wasn't, but there happened to be a pile of magazines in the *one* rocker where my husband was about to sit. "John, all this CRAP (*word change again*) is yours! I'm gonna haul it all out to the dumpster when you fall asleep!" And, I'm pretty sure she did.

I'm telling you, they were downright *mean* to one another. I was a nervous wreck by the time we left, each and every time. My husband assured me that the two of them were devoted to each other, that this was their way of showing their affection. HA! I think that's part of the reason my marriage to him didn't work out—he started showing *his* affection in the same way as his uncle.

My grandma used to say, "Take care of your thoughts when you are alone, and take care of your words when you are with people." I never once heard my grandma cuss or raise her voice. I'm not sure where my mother picked up the habit of screaming and cussing. I am ashamed to say that it is my own worst habit, to raise my voice when I start getting upset. I struggle with it less as I've aged, but my poor son probably has hearing damage because of my rants.

My current husband would *never* tolerate someone yelling, fussing, or cussing all the time. He has definitely helped me curb my temper. Don't misunderstand; I still get mad. However, I have learned more appropriate ways to express my displeasure.

Of course, I'd like to blame my temper on my mom *and* my dad, but the reality is, we are all responsible for our own lives. The constant harping at one another, finding fault with one another, never showing kindness with a word or deed ... All these mentally abusive things are bad enough, but when you also add in throwing objects, and physical abuse ... Well, all I can say is that I had plenty of examples of what *not* to do.

I think the maddest I ever made my mom—and believe me, I could push her buttons—was when she used her all-famous cuss word: S**tfire! This word had to have been my mom's favorite word of all time because she used it all the time. "Well, s**tfire, that coffee is hot." "S**tfire, Dorenda, haven't you finished the dishes yet!?" "That's just a bunch of s**tfire that he said to me today." I think you get the gist.

On this particular day, my mom blurted out the "S**tfire," and I interrupted her tirade with, "Well, *that* would sure hurt to s**t fire instead of poop!" Oh, she did *not* think that was funny!

Sometimes, we, kids, would accidentally get in the middle of one of my mom's and her current husband's arguments. Believe me, we were very inventive on ways to avoid such scenes—hiding under tables, sneaking outside, turning the volume up on the TV, or trying to run to our bedroom. I can remember my brother trying to distract one or the other parent with a fake, "There's someone on the phone for you, Mom."

I wasn't always diligent in being aware of a fight brewing, and sometimes, I wasn't smart enough to get out of the way. One morning, I was eating cereal at the built-in L-shaped dinette in our kitchen. I was on the bench against the wall, sitting behind the table. My mom started fussing with Chick (husband #6). I'm not really sure why I was so oblivious, probably had my head stuck in my usual escape mechanism, a book, but all Hades broke loose before I suddenly came out from my trance.

My path of escape was cut off by the two adults who had moved their "disagreement" into the kitchen. I can't even tell you what the fight was about. *All* the fights sounded the same—lots of name-calling, cussing, screaming, and threats. This one was escalating fast. I decided my best bet was to crawl under the table and try to sneak behind the chairs. Turns out, this was not the best strategy because it put me smack dab between the two combatants. Next thing I knew, my mom grabbed the percolator, full of hot coffee, and flung it at Chick. The thing had been plugged in, but as she jerked it off the counter, the plug gave way, throwing off her aim enough that the coffee pot hit me instead of Chick.

Luckily, it did not spill out, and luckier still, it did not hit my face. One learns to dodge pretty fast in a home where it's "strike first, ask questions later." My forearm took the brunt of the hot pot, and I suffered a severe third-degree burn. It didn't slow down the fight, however; they then started fighting over whose fault it was that I got hit. The important thing was … the coffee pot still worked.

Lots of kids in my era got spankings or "switched." Some really diabolical parents would even make their kids go get the switch off a tree. Growing up mostly in Oklahoma, we didn't have a lot of trees, so my mother improvised by using a belt. To this day, the hair raises on the back of my neck when I hear someone snap a belt. If you don't know what I'm talking about, *good*. The belt used was nothing like today's little flimsy elastic or plastic things. Nope, these were 2" thick leather belts with a steel buckle.

Mom would hold the two ends of the belt in one hand, the looped end in the other, then bring the two hands closer together to create a gap. Then, she would jerk the two ends apart, which caused the gap to *snap* shut. I tell you, it was a *horrifying* sound to a kid that knows the belt is coming for them. I have no idea how many "whuppings" I got as a kid, but I do know that I have an aversion to belts to this day. Sometimes, the whippings only left red marks for a day or so, but sometimes the belt left welt marks and bloody stripes.

Honestly? As bad as the belt beatings were, I preferred those to my mom's slaps and hits. If she were in a really bad rage, especially if she had been drinking, the slaps and hits would continue until you could escape (told you I learned how to dodge).

I know she "disciplined" my brother until he was old enough to take the belt away from her. It was probably about that time that she stopped using the belt on me, although the slap beatings continued. She never used the belt on either of my two younger sisters, thank God, nor do I ever remember her slapping either of them. Truthfully, my sister, Jo, never did anything wrong. I am *not* exaggerating. She did as she was told; she never talked back; she was kind and sweet to our littlest sister. Even as an adult, about the worst thing my sister, Jo, has ever said to or about anyone is, "She's being a pill!"

The worst beating I EVER got from Mom happened the night before my wedding, at age 19, my last night in her home. It was so bad that I called my fiancé around 3 a.m. to tell him I loved him, and to say I was sorry. I honestly didn't think I would survive the night, to even show up at the church the next morning. My mother had been heavily drinking, as had Chick. They were both furious with me for inviting my dad to my wedding. I took several blows to my face and head before I promised I would ask my brother to walk me down the aisle, that I wouldn't let Dad do it. That seemed to appease them. So, I went into my bedroom, which I shared with my sister, Jo, and thought the worst was over.

Regretfully, the drinking continued, and their tempers escalated over the next hour. Sometime after midnight, they burst into the bedroom, throwing on the lights. Both had beer bottles, and proceeded to beat my legs and torso through the bed coverings. I remember my mother yelling, "Don't touch her face!" She had enough sense to realize she didn't want others to see the results of their abuse.

It is solely by the grace of God, and my grandma's intervention, that the beating was stopped before any more than bruising and lumps could occur. There was no sleep for me the rest of that night, and I slipped out of the house at the break of dawn, going straight to the church. The whole wedding was a blur. Even when I look at the wedding pictures, I truly don't remember any of it.

It's an understatement to say alcoholism is terrible for families, but it pales in comparison to drug abuse. So I count myself lucky that this was the worst thing I had to contend with while growing up. Mom's behavior could be blamed on the drinking, but I really don't accept the flimsy excuse when people say, "Well, I was drunk."

When she wasn't drinking, Mom was basically a responsible parent who always found a way to feed and clothe us. I have a very strong "pull yourself up by your bootstraps" mentality, and I attribute that to my mom. But, when she was drinking, it was often miserable.

I didn't appreciate it at the time, but my mom was teaching me a very important life lesson when she was drinking—it definitely made me a stronger person. Drinking led to a loss of control for my mother; perhaps that is why she was so controlling in other aspects of her life.

When You Try to Control Everything, You Gain Nothing

I didn't see or understand it at the time, but my mom had a very domineering personality. Perhaps that was her survival mechanism. So much of her life was out of her control, so she attempted to govern every aspect of her children's lives.

There is a difference between being a "controlling, governing" parent and an "attentive" parent. My brother rebelled in his teens, running around with friends that I would have classified as hoodlums. However, this is the viewpoint of a little sister; I'm sure when Rodney reads this, he will take exception to my calling Billy, Hugh, Keith, and the others anything less than fine upstanding citizens.

It's a good thing we lived in such a small town because the skirmishes with the law that Rodney and his cohorts had were minor. Mom was always able to bail him out—*not* literally; my brother had no juvenile record or real trouble. It could have been so much worse because, for a while, my brother was following in my mother's footsteps—drinking, partying, being abusive—and yet, he always held a good job and provided a living for himself and his family. I'm not sure if I have my Aunt Nerva Jewel to thank or if it was divine intervention, but something turned Rodney's life around in early adulthood, thank God. To this day, I am absolutely positive my brother would do anything in the world for my sisters or me. I might have said it before in this book, but it bears repeating: my brother, Rodney, is the Godliest man I know.

I think my mom overlooked a lot of Rodney's behavior because "he's a boy," and in her experience, one can't control a male. Not so when it came to me. She attempted to run every part of my existence—my friends, my activities in and out of school, my jobs, clothing, even my hair. Here is a glimpse into my childhood, from about the fifth grade forward:

"Dorenda, you had better have all the dishes washed, dried, and put away before school, or you'll be spending the day here doing it!"

"Dorenda, did you vacuum the living room and hall?"

"Dorenda, did you get that load of ironing done?"

Whether it was the dishes, the vacuuming, or the ironing, I knew I had better have it done, or I would be kept out of school that day. In elementary school, the Truancy Officer regularly visited our house. I was coached by my mom, on

152

threat of a beating, to always cough and say how sick I felt. By junior high, I knew what I had to do in order to be allowed to go to school. I was up before dawn every single morning, doing the chores that I could do quietly and vacuuming as everyone else started to rise. I tried hard to walk out the door before I could be stopped, saying, "Bye, have a good day."

When we lived on C Street in Altus, we had a problem with roaches. To this day, I am OCD about never leaving a dirty dish in the sink or unsealed food on the counter. My mother hated roaches as well, so she decided that every morning I was to take every plate, cup, bowl, and glass out of the cabinets and rewash/dry them, "just in case any roaches ran over them last night."

And if she ever pulled a dish out of the cabinet that wasn't quite clean (Lord, that dried egg wouldn't come off!), she would then unload *all* the dishes, pots and pans, silverware, and cooking paraphernalia out onto the kitchen table, screaming at me the entire time that it was my own fault. Those were definitely days that I would miss school. Good thing too, or it might have been hard to write anything with my "pruney" dishpan hands.

One of the useful skills that came out of this was that I learned how to iron properly. I know; this is an obsolete skill with today's fabrics. I did such a good job that Rodney paid me a nickel for every one of his shirts—never mind that it took me a quarter-hour to actually iron one properly. At least it was something to look forward to.

Once I left home, the memories of all my chores faded. I tried to be more philosophical about it, to try and justify why my mother seemed to target me. After all, Jo was three years younger, so she couldn't do it; Rodney was always working a job, and Mom worked most nights. So, I was the logical choice. Years later, it was my sister-in-law, Terri, who confirmed, "Dorenda, you were an unpaid slave. Your mom did that to keep you under her thumb so you couldn't ever get a real job and leave. You were a real-life Cinderella!" So much for my rose-colored view of that part of my life.

School was another matter. I *loved* school. I *loved* tests. I know; I was a nerd before nerds were cool. I *loved* my teachers, at least all but Mrs. Schmidt, the geography teacher at Falcon Elementary—she was mean with that ruler of hers. School was not just my daily escape from home, but I also knew early on that a good education was going to be my ticket out; I had to be patient. Again, my mother inadvertently taught me a valuable lesson: without a good education, you will never get a decent, good-paying job.

In the sixth grade, at Washington Elementary, I tried out for the cheerleading squad. I was very good. Of course, it was nothing like today's cheerleaders who have had years of gymnastics, dance, and professional training; I speak from experience here because three of my granddaughters participate in this sport, and one excels in gymnastics. They have even competed nationally. My level of expertise was nothing compared to today's gymnasts and cheerleaders. However, I was chosen for the squad, and I was ecstatic. My favorite teacher, Mrs. Fox, pulled me aside and asked if my mother could afford my uniform. Well, dang it ... I hadn't thought of that!

Not to worry, Mrs. Fox said she would take care of it if Mom couldn't, that some of the girls from last year had their uniforms for sale. Okay, beaming smile back in place on my face. I was so excited to go home that day to tell Mom I had made the squad, and that Mrs. Fox was going to get me a uniform.

Who knows what went through my mother's mind. Maybe she was embarrassed about the charity. All I know is that she showed up at school the next day to tell the principal I was not allowed to participate because she couldn't take me to and from the football games. He assured her that the cheerleading sponsor would do so, as she did with all the girls. Nope, that was not acceptable to my mom. I was off the squad, and that was that.

From that point on, I never asked my mother for permission to participate in any extra-curricular activity. If it was something I really wanted to do, I paid for it myself and made it happen. It only became an issue when things took place outside regular school hours.

I have always loved English, mainly because of the reading part, but truthfully, I even love grammar, especially diagramming sentences. Please hang with me, because my grammar skills have kept me employed through the years. In the eleventh grade, my American Literature teacher, Mrs. Whitworth, convinced me to compete in the SWIM meet. No, I wasn't an athlete. (I actually didn't learn to swim until I was in my 50s.) SWIM was the Southwestern Oklahoma State University Interscholastic Meet, held every year in Weatherford, Oklahoma, for the top high school scholars in a number of disciplines. Somehow, Mrs. Whitworth convinced my mother to allow me to go with her so I could compete on one fine Saturday morning.

I took first place honors in the American Literature contest. The next year, I competed for Mrs. Sifford and took first place in English Literature. I fell in love with the SW campus and the town of Weatherford. It would have been my college of choice if things had worked out differently in my life.

These two awards should have made my mother proud of me, should have made her realize I was capable of doing more than selling encyclopedias for her at the air base. It was a calculated risk on my part to try and convince her of my worth. It backfired, however, and my mother became more determined than ever that I would *not* be going to college. She never once acknowledged any awards or honors I received, even when I gave a graduation address at my junior high school, Northeast. It was only after I left home that she actually started showing any pride in my accomplishments, such as college graduations.

In spite of her lack of support, and her interference in my attendance, I did well in school, an A–B student. In my tenth grade year, I took the ACT and scored a composite 27, which put me on the radar of a number of colleges. This score wouldn't compare these days, but this was before ACT or SAT prep classes were available. I received a very surprising call one evening from Oklahoma Baptist University, offering me a fully-paid scholarship for all four years. I was very honest with the counselor: I had no transportation to Tulsa, nor did I have any money for room and board. He indicated that the dorm and meal plan were included, and OBU would help me find a work-study position for all my incidentals. I was ready to yell, "Sign me up!"

However, I knew I would have to get my mom's approval … How else would I get to Tulsa? So, I asked the counselor to call me the next evening, to give me a chance to talk to my mother. Oh, that conversation did *not* go well. "You're not going to college! No one needs college! You have to go to work!"

I argued with my mom until she got a fanatical look in her eye. When she said, "That'll happen over my dead body, or yours, girly-girl," I knew it was time to shut up.

Nonetheless, I absolutely knew I would definitely be going to college, even if it were only the local community college in Altus, the one I could walk to. (Remember? No car.) I dreaded the OBU call the next evening, but I was resigned that I had to turn it down.

I didn't even get a chance. As I answered the extension in the hallway, my mother answered the one in the kitchen. I don't know if she had been drinking, but I'd like to use that as an excuse. She cussed the guy out, told him I was *not* going to OBU, and that if he ever called our house again, she would file charges. No further offers came from OBU.

My mother also threw away any college responses I received in the mail, including partial scholarship offers from Southwestern for my SWIM wins. When I graduated from high school at age 17, I was required to give any gift money directly to my mother and Chick "as payment for room and board, now that you are out of school."

That was a control effort on their part to ensure that I did not ever leave home, that I give up on the idea of going to college. I briefly tried to find another place to live but lacked the confidence to think I could make it on my own. Instead, I sucked it up and bargained to be allowed to attend the local community college. They ultimately agreed, as long as I continued with all my chores *and* paid $100 board every month to my mother, they would allow me to go to Altus Junior College. I don't think they thought I would get any scholarships to AJC, but I did; between that and the work-study position, I was able to fully pay for my own education.

I often wondered why my mother referred to me as her "problem child." I assumed it was because I was sarcastic, a smart-aleck. If I heard, "You better shut that smart mouth right now, or I'm gonna shut it for you," once, I heard it a gazillion times.

I never smoked, never tried drugs, never even wanted to drink, didn't have sex until I met my husband, so no unwanted pregnancies, *and* I made good grades. In hindsight, though, I believe Mom thought of me as a problem because I didn't kowtow to her wishes. She did not want things to change. I served a purpose in the household, and there was no one else who would fulfill these obligations if I left.

It was obvious Mom did not value schooling or a degree of any kind. In her own experience, an eighth-grade education was good enough. It had never stopped her, as far as she could tell. She had honed her skills of scheming and conniving through the "school of hard knocks," so why do anything else?

She wasn't always like that; I remember her being proud of my winning a bookmark design contest at the Altus Air Force Base Library, when I was in probably the third grade. The Library printed up hundreds of the bookmark—a worm holding a book with a college cap on its head (a "bookworm")—to give away whenever someone checked out a book. My mom went in and took dozens so she could hand them out and brag, "My daughter, Dorenda, drew this and won the contest out of thousands of entries." In truth, it could have been the ONLY entry; I don't know. I simply know how good it felt that my mom was proud of me, her problem child.

She and Buck also attended my first college graduation for my bachelor's degree at Cameron University in Lawton, Oklahoma. It was the town my husband and I moved to after marrying, about an hour from Altus. Perhaps her views of education had mellowed in the three years I had been gone.

A Damaged Moral Compass

Actions speak so much louder than words, and parents should realize this. My mother always told us, "I love each of you equally." However, her actions belied this over and over again. My brother, because he was a boy, was favored and allowed extra privileges that my sisters and I were not. My sister, Jo, because she was so docile and agreeable, was definitely my mother's favorite, at least until our youngest sister, Taffy, came along.

The favoritism showed up in daily treatment as well as at Christmas. When I was in grade school, my mother forgot to give me a Christmas present one year. As I sat there with no presents to open, she finally noticed and took one of the five dolls my sister had received, saying, "Oh, this doll is for you; I just labeled it wrong."

What was even worse (and boy, I sure hate to admit this), weeks before Christmas, I had snuck into the closet where she hid the presents prior to wrapping. I saw one of the dolls was a gorgeous wedding doll, complete with a trousseau; all the other dolls were baby dolls, so I knew the wedding doll was for me, her oldest daughter. Nope, I was given one of the baby dolls when my mom realized I had not received anything. I think there was definitely a lesson to be learned in that incident—sneaky nosiness does not pay off.

Even as an adult, the favoritism was undeniable. One Christmas, before my son was born, we went to my mom's house to exchange presents. I remember both my sisters receiving elaborate gifts—can't tell you what they were now, but trust me. This was understandable because they both still lived at home. When my husband opened his, it was a flannel shirt that would not have fit a young boy, let alone a 200-lb 6-foot tall man. I was fuming because it was insulting.

However, once I opened my own gift, also in torn packaging, my anger turned to being flabbergasted. I received a Presto Burger maker ... including pieces of raw hamburger where someone had evidently already tried using it! This incident served to remind us: it's not the gift that counts; it's the thought behind it. It was evident what my mother thought of us.

My mom did not always display model adult behavior. Besides her lying, she was also a thief. I'm not talking about her stealing money or anything of value at any of her jobs. After all, this was the woman who taught us to always be on time, never leave work early, and give more than a day's work for a day's pay. No, what she stole was weird stuff and always when we were with her.

For example, if we were waiting for the doctor in the exam room, she would stuff her purse full of the cotton balls or Q-tips from the jars on the counter. I am still flummoxed as to why she would do this. I never once remember her using said objects. At restaurants, she would take all the sugar and jelly packets that were on the table. Perhaps we used those, but again, I don't recall ever seeing them at home. I even remember touring some new mobile homes at a trailer lot once upon a time, and my mom removing one of the smaller décor items—a string of beads holding a shower curtain back—and stuffing it in her purse.

I have no logical explanation for this behavior; perhaps one of you will have an answer to why a mostly honest person would do any of these things. Was she bipolar? Was she trying to prove she could do it without getting caught? Who knows!

Okay, enough of that ... Whew, almost makes me break out in hives when I dredge all that up! Suffice it to say, if my mom did nothing else as a parent, she served as a bad example that I could strive to avoid.

Lessons I Learned on Parenting

I can't speak for my brother or sister, but I absolutely know my mother's parenting skills affected my own. The six common traits of children of alcoholics are:[4]

low self-esteem

constantly seeking approval

fear of authority

fear of abandonment

isolation

a victim perspective

---

[4] Buddy T, "Characteristics of Adult Children of Alcoholics," Verywell Mind (Verywell Mind, November 5, 2021), https://www.verywellmind.com/common-traits-of-adult-children-of-alcoholics-66557.

Perhaps because my mom was a functioning alcoholic, my siblings and I overcame or never had most of these six traits. Although, if I am totally honest with myself, I continue to fight a fear of abandonment, but that may be due not only to my mother's alcoholism but also the revolving door of fathers, physical abuse, and the unfaithfulness of my first husband.

I also know that I am extremely uncomfortable around a person who has had too much to drink. I am on edge, defensive, feeling like my "fight or flight" mechanism is in overdrive. I have no issues in a social situation where people are moderately drinking; it's only when my companions have gone beyond the point of "feeling good" or "slightly tipsy" that I am anything *but* feeling good.

Early in my married life, I read a book entitled *Adult Children of Alcoholics*.[5] It explained so much of my own behavior and solidified my determination to no longer let it control my life.

- Did I have to guess what normal behavior was? Yes, that's why I thought everyone's life *should* have been an episode of "Father Knows Best."

- Did I have difficulty having fun? Certainly, after all, one of us in the household had to be the adult.

- Did I take myself too seriously? So much so that to this day, I sometimes have trouble realizing someone is teasing.

---

[5] Janet Geringer Woititz, *Adult Children of Alcoholics* (Deerfield Beach, FL: Health Communications, 1990).

- Did I overreact to changes over which I have no control? Good Lord, *yes*, and to this day, it is a trait I have to dial back. (Ask my husband.) Self-control is vital in a world that is out of control.

- Was I impulsive? Yep, but nowadays, I try to make impulsive decisions about having fun.

- Was I extremely loyal, even in the face of evidence that the loyalty is undeserved? Well, why do you think I held on to a 21-year marriage where unhappiness had repeatedly occurred?

- Did I constantly seek approval and affirmation? Again, this is a character flaw that I still try hard to overcome.

- Did I improperly deal with displays of temper or violence? Most definitely, sometimes reacting with my own temper, but mostly developing a fear of that person or bully.

- Did I own blame, constantly apologizing as if I were responsible for every mistake? Wow, this one really hits me upside the head. And, I hate that I passed this trait on to my son, the habit of saying, "I'm sorry," all the time, even when I bear no responsibility.

As for my own parenting (and believe me, I made *plenty* of mistakes), I tried hard to be consistent, fair, and firm. This even carried over into the classroom, where I taught for 30 years. Did I exhibit tough love at times? Was I sometimes too demanding, too impatient, with too high expectations? Did I yell too much, too loudly, too often? The answer isn't possibly or probably; it's definitely. For that, I apologize. I can only hope that my son knows where my heart is, and that he is more forgiving of my faults than I was of my own mother.

Despite all the things I did wrong, I tried with all my heart to be one of three places at all times for my son: in front of him to encourage and cheer him on, behind him to let him know I always had his back, or next to him so that he was never walking alone. He's now in his 40s, and I hope he knows he can still count on me to be one of those three places.

I started this book by saying I loved my mom, but I didn't like her. After this chapter, perhaps you can understand why. But I also told you that I realized too late that my mom was trying to be the best person she knew how to be. It has been in my later years that I recognized my mom didn't inspire us by being perfect. Instead, she inspired us by how she dealt with her own imperfections.

I will leave this chapter with a quote from Ann Landers: "It is not what you do for your children, but what you have taught them to do for themselves, that will make them successful human beings."

By that standard, my mother did all right by us kids, even if some of her examples were "what *not* to do."

This was a heavy chapter, so I promise this next one will be much lighter. In fact, it's only "skin-deep." 😀

Chapter 7

Beauty Is as Beauty Does

"Pretty Woman" by Roy Orbison

I've already established that my mother was beautiful. A few more of her photos through the ages will be scattered throughout this chapter. Even in her later years, Mom was always a beauty for whatever her age was at the time.

She knew she was beautiful. Sometimes it's better for a pretty girl to be unaware that she is pretty. I'm quite sure that my mom's beauty and outgoing personality cost her numerous female friendships. If I were to name any lifelong friends of my mom's, it would be her sister, Nerva Jewel, and a cousin by the name of Mary Anne. These two hung in there because the Lowrys always believed "Family is forever, through thick and thin."

There were a few other female friends whose names occasionally popped up—Trixie, Dolly, Peggy, Joanne—but these women's friendships were as short-lived as some of my mother's relationships with men.

Figure 60 Mom through the ages with some of her girlfriends (Trixie, bottom pic).

In looking at photos of Mom with various girlfriends, I don't think I am being biased in saying that she was always the prettiest of the two, or of the group. Mom believed her greatest asset was her looks; it wasn't, but I am convinced that is what *she* believed. As a result, she put great stock in beauty and appearance. This invariably had an effect on me, but more on that later.

Mom had an amazing figure. Her legs were gorgeous, always slim and well-shaped. High heels took their toll as the years passed, messing up her feet and knees. She was always well endowed; I lamented missing out on this particular trait as I grew into womanhood.

Figure 61 Mom, circa the late '50s.

She had an innate sense of style that allowed her to showcase this particular feature of her anatomy without appearing crass or trashy. My mother was always well dressed. She always had make-up on, not a lot, but at least mascara and lipstick, usually red. Her skin was soft and blemish-free with barely enough tan shade to never require liquid makeup. Powder was about the only thing I remember her using on her face. She always dressed stylishly and favored suits in the last couple of decades of her life.

Figure 62 Mom in the '50s.

Two of my mother's most unique beauty features were her teeth and her hair. Unfortunately, she was destined to lose both, and not when she turned 80, as happens with most of us.

Whether it was the hard times while she was growing up, or ignorance on the part of Mom's family, dental care was nonexistent. Mom had a gap in her two front teeth—which I also inherited—but that wasn't the issue. After all, some of Hollywood's most gorgeous women have gaps—Brigitte Bardot, Madonna, Lauren Hutton, to name a few. No, it was the poor dental health that caused my mom to give up her teeth completely. Sometime in the 1960s, I think, Mom had a full set of false teeth. The gap was gone, but so were her happiest and most natural smiles, in my opinion.

She had gorgeous, thick, raven hair for many years, but alas, female baldness is hereditary in our family. It started

170

making its appearance as Mom turned 40, before she even had a chance to start turning grey. She relied more and more on wigs. She had several different hairpieces, made into various styles—long and wavy with bangs, a beehive, layered curls, and even a pageboy. Most were black because that was her natural hair color, but at least one blonde wig was in her arsenal.

I remember a funny story when I was in grade school. We were in Central Pharmacy in Altus, the drug store we always used when I was growing up. I was fascinated that this little store had a loudspeaker system ... "Customer waiting in Aisle 3" or "Customer needs assistance at the soda fountain." My sister, Jo, and I were in the toy aisle while Mom filled a prescription. We immediately found something we thought we couldn't live without, so I promptly went up to the cashier and asked her to go on the loudspeaker and to "Please ask Jo McGee to meet her children in the toy aisle."

The cashier was up on a raised platform, so she could obviously see much more of the store than I could from a child's angle. Plus, I'm pretty sure she didn't want to start the habit of making announcements per the requests of kids. So, she asked me what my mother was wearing and what color her hair was. I was a little flummoxed at this interrogation, but I quickly rallied and said, "She's wearing a purple dress and has black hair. NO! Wait, she has blonde hair today!"

Needless to say, the cashier never made the announcement, much to my disappointment, because she was now convinced I was pulling a prank. And, to add salt to the wound, my mom didn't even consider buying the toy my sister and I had found. All in all, a very dissatisfying trip to the pharmacy.

Figure 63 A Glamour Shot Session when Mom was in her 50s.

My mother's vanity with her hair eventually cost her one of her best attributes. She had a standing weekly appointment with LaVerne, her hairdresser, there in Altus. LaVerne would "rat" my mother's hair to make it poof up for the beehives she wore. Ratting one's hair is literally putting "rats" or tangles in it; it's also called backcombing or teasing. Eventually, those tangles have to be combed out, and when this happens, hair is actually pulled out of the scalp. If my mother weren't already genetically destined to go bald, this backcombing practice would have done the trick.

In addition, as we now know, the constant use of hats or wigs kills hair follicles and causes baldness. Mother had very little hair on her head by the time she was in her 60s. She was so embarrassed that she slept with a turban, immediately donning a wig as soon as she awoke.

Throughout her life, people described my mom as "beautiful," "gorgeous," "prettiest gal in Oklahoma." She never lost her desire to appear at her best, whether it was sitting in her home as she aged or, especially, if she were going out to dinner or even shopping. The wig would be in place, she would wear a nice outfit, and lipstick would be the crowning touch. She always asked for a new sweater or a new outfit for Christmas. She still loved nice clothes and loved to dress up. That never changed as long as she lived.

Figure 64 Mother in one of her favorite pantsuits.

Sorry to admit, this did *not* wear off on me. No, I'm not one of those people that jump out of bed and head to Walmart in my sweats or pj's (thank God!); however, I stopped wearing my suits and heels when I retired from teaching. Never one for a lot of make-up, I ceased using anything but occasional lipstick in my 50s. I have always been more of a "natural look" person because it fits my lifestyle of outdoor activities. Regretfully (or not), my looks are NOT the first thing people will use to describe me, as they always have with my mother.

Mom's fixation on beauty carried over to her parenting. She not only wanted to appear at her best at all times, but she also wanted her daughters to do so. It was a common thing, back in the '50s, to dress one's daughters in colors and clothing like the mother's, albeit in a more child-acceptable style. My sister and I often had matching outfits, especially for holidays or family photos.

Figure 65 Jo and me with matching outfits; me with spit-curls, and lucky Rodney.

My hair is naturally wavy, not curly, but definitely frizzy when it's humid, and very definitely unruly. My sister, Jo, has always had straight hair. Mom would spit-curl (yes, you read that right) our hair using bobby pins. I hated sleeping in these. I think that's where my beauty rebellion might have started. By the time I was in fourth grade, I refused to dress like my sister or my mother. I was developing my own personality, and it was more along the lines of "tomboy." I was happiest in shorts and shirts, not dresses. Because I no longer tolerated my mother curling my hair, she kept my hair cut so it would be manageable. Occasionally she would force me to get a permanent. I would walk in with hair that was about a foot long, but the permanent was so tight I'd walk out with my head looking like a steel wool pad.

Mother retaliated against my tomboyish looks and behavior by introducing me and my sister, Jo, as "the smart one and the pretty one" throughout our young lives. As a parent, my mother had no idea how affecting this categorizing was to my sister and me. I know for a fact I became convinced that because I was "the smart one," I was not pretty, not in the least. This had a devastating effect on me when I was in high school as far as my social life was concerned.

Sadly, on the opposite side of the coin, my sister, Jo, has always seemed to believe she is not smart. The reality is she is one of the wisest people I know, despite her lack of book education.

One could argue that Mom's calling me "the smart one" caused me to focus more on school and value education. That would be very correct. You see, for every negative, there is a positive.

And, I know, as an adult looking back on that time, I was never "homely." However, those junior high and high school years were super tough on a young girl with no self-confidence. Mom didn't help any with her harping, "Dorenda, get your head outta that book! Boys don't like girls that are too smart!"

In the early '70s, straight hair, short skirts, and bell-bottoms were all the rage. I'm sure I faced the same arguments as my friends when Mother would vehemently declare, "You are NOT going to school with that short of a dress!"

Fate looked kindly on me because my sister-in-law, Terri, gave me a lot of her dresses—and they all came from Jack's Rose, my favorite expensive store. I am 5'7", and Terri barely hits 5'. What was a respectable length on her, was perfectly in fashion for me. She was the BEST sister-in-law in the world because she would intervene, saying, "Jo, it looks fine. Leave her alone."

I spent hours rolling my wavy hair on tin cans or ironing my hair to try straightening it. However, my self-confidence was further shattered as Mom would snidely remark, "Your hair looks horrible. You need to cut it off or wear one of my wigs!" (Like *that* would ever have happened!)

Sometimes, my mother's vanity was embarrassing. For example, the two of us were walking down the street one day, on the town square of Altus. A couple of boys—guys I recognized from high school—whistled as the two of us walked by. My mother, quite loudly and confidently, said, "Now, Boys, you *know* I'm too old for you." I was mortified. One might excuse it by assuming she was joking, but I assure you, she was not.

In my junior year of Altus High School, Mr. Dial, bless his heart, tried his best to instill assurance and poise in me and one of my best friends, Kathy Jones. He would say things like, "The prettiest girls are always the last ones to be asked on dates because the boys are scared they'll be turned down." He convinced me to compete in a beauty contest for Miss DECA (Distributive Education Clubs of America). Visions of my suddenly being hailed as a beauty, as my mother was, danced in my head.

Mom was ecstatic that I was finally taking an interest in my appearance. We had a limited budget, certainly no funds for an evening gown. I so wanted to go buy an outfit at *the* store where all the "rich girls" shopped, Jack's Rose, but that was out of the question. Instead, my ever-resourceful mother contacted one of her insurance customers, an older lady who had had a very active social life at one time, and had closets full of evening wear. I wish I could remember her name. I was tall and skinny, so I had no problem fitting into this society matron's gowns. Mom bought three, so I'd have one for each of the junior-senior proms as well. Lesson learned—never let something as silly as a lack of money keep you from reaching for the stars.

Fast forward to the evening of the beauty contest. Again, I thought I had suddenly transformed into a dazzling diva overnight, and I waltzed onto the stage along with about fifteen other girls, who all probably thought the same thing. As Mr. Dial announced each girl's name, she stepped forward out of the line, then back again. We had been coached to stand straight and tall, smile, and face the audience the entire time the introductions were made. I was probably number eleven or twelve, and wore a sheer yellow, empire-waisted gown. I was so scared and nervous; I was ready to fall off that stage.

Once the last girl was introduced, a hush fell over the auditorium; Mr. Dial asked each DECA member to fill in their ballots and pass them to the end of the aisle. All of a sudden, the silence was broken by one boy who shouted, "Don't vote for the girl in the yellow dress—she's flat-chested!"

Yes, I was the *only* girl in a yellow dress, and yes, I was flat-chested—told you I didn't inherit many of my mom's attributes. My ears started ringing, shutting out the laughter or further comments, and I'm sure I blazed scarlet

... which is *so* unappealing in yellow. I don't remember anything else, not leaving the stage or even going home with my mom. It was a humiliating experience and one I would *never* repeat again. Only contests of a cerebral nature would be entered by me from that point on.

Unlike my contemporaries, I was not allowed to date until I turned 16, my junior year of high school. I really don't know why I'm complaining, because it wasn't as if boys were knocking the doors down to ask me out. My childhood "boyfriend" was David Kimball. He was as awkward as I was, even in high school. The boy I most liked in high school, Charles Bello, was not as kind as he could have been. Lord, why don't teenage girls realize how immature boys are at that age!? That's about the sum total of guys I dated in high school.

Honestly, I didn't encourage guys to ask me out; I was fairly introverted, to begin with, and I never knew what shenanigans my mother would pull. "No, you're going to be babysitting Peggy's kids Saturday night, not going out." It was easier not to accept a date, to begin with, than to have to explain later.

By the time I was attending junior college, I had started dating others, but dates did not always go well. I had a very severe curfew, even at age 18. One night, after arriving at my house well before the 10 p.m. curfew, my date and I sat in his car talking. I'm guessing the clock struck 10, but neither of us noticed. My mother came out of the house, in her robe and nightwear, drunk as a skunk, cussing and screaming. She threw her beer bottle at the poor kid's windshield, cracked it, and scared the living daylights out of both of us! I jumped out of the car, trying to calm my mother, and he was doing his best to start his car to escape. It would *not* turn over! Ultimately, Chick and I pushed as the kid got it started, driving away, never to return.

Lessons Learned About Beauty

External beauty is a wonderful thing to have. I would argue, the most discriminated group on the face of this earth is not a particular race or religion; it is ugly women, no matter what race or religion. An unattractive woman finds it harder to get a job, get a mate, or get a life—no matter how smart, how well educated, how personable she might be. Attractive women are more readily accepted into social situations, employment, and even friendships. This is my opinion, not a proven scientific fact that I have researched.

That said, external beauty can also be a burden, especially if the person who is blessed with said beauty is 1) aware they are attractive and 2) believes this beauty is their only or most important attribute. Mom definitely fell into this category, not realizing she had so much more to offer until later in life, as her beauty began to fade.

I count myself lucky that I never depended on my external package to carry the day. I don't *think* I was ever described as "but she has a good personality;" however, I wouldn't mind if I were.

Early on, I realized that a good education would be my key to success, my way out of the kind of life my mother lived, *not* my beauty. My schooling was going to prepare me for a respectable career, one where I would never have to be dependent on another person.

Although I would have liked to have finished my Ph.D., I am most proud of my education, especially since I put myself through school. Please don't misunderstand; I still have a fair dose of vanity, and like most women, I really do want to hear my husband occasionally say, "Wow, you look great!" Compliments are always appreciated, especially when they encompass my creations in photography or writing.

Somewhere along the line, I read that compliments should be about "the person" not the objects. For example, your friend might be sporting a new red dress. Instead of saying, "Gorgeous red dress," you *should* say, "You make that dress look gorgeous! Red is definitely your color!" I always try to remember that and rephrase my compliments to others accordingly.

Not everyone knows how to give compliments, and false ones are worse than keeping one's mouth shut. I recall one special event where my photography was displayed throughout the event venue. Don't be too impressed—it was not an exhibit showcasing my work, but my work was used to enhance the event. I was so proud and looked forward to hearing my family members "ooh" and "aah." Instead, one of them said, "That camera of yours sure takes a great picture." It was not only a poor compliment; it came close to being an insult. So, I've also learned to strive for excellence for myself, for my own pleasure, not to try and impress anyone else.

The incident where I could not afford a new evening gown, but my mom found a way for me to have one that was at least "new to me" … that lives in my memory as one of the best traits of my mother. She never accepted defeat; she always found a way to make things happen. If I learned nothing else from my mom, this was a trait I would do well to emulate.

Nevertheless, the most important lesson I learned while growing up with a beautiful mother is that internal beauty is far more significant than good looks. To be kind, to be appreciative and grateful, to never take for granted good fortune, good friends, or good family ... these are the truly vital aspects of one's being.

Mother certainly had more going for her than her looks, but she didn't always realize that. As I'll disclose in the next chapter, her humor and creativity kept all of us, kids, entertained. Yes, kangaroos, vampires, and even wet linens were all included in her repertoire of tricks.

Chapter 8

The Mother We Were Proud to Know

"Never Grow Up" by Taylor Swift

I am ashamed to admit that I never truly appreciated everything I share in this chapter until after my mom passed away. These are the traditions unique to our family, initiated by my mother. I am positive these were not behaviors handed down by my grandparents. My grandma lived with us, and most of these were as new to her as they were to us kids. As I think of these many quirky things, I once again realize how creative my mother was. None of these required a great deal of money or preparation. Oftentimes they were spur-of-the-moment ideas that brought laughter into our lives and, thus, became a tradition.

Mr. Kangaroo

One of my earliest memories was what my brother and I refer to as the "Mr. Kangaroo Ruse." These were the days of landlines, no cell phones. As a matter of fact, it was so long ago, the phone itself had to be *dialed*—no punch numbers. Instead of tennis elbow, I guess people had finger exertion.

There were no "long-distance phone plans." If one made a long-distance phone call—meaning any calls outside the city limits—the phone company charged extra on one's monthly bill. This was always to be avoided; the monthly bill was bad enough. Today's equivalent would be using more data on one's cell phone than is covered in the basic plan; the overage charges are outrageous. So too, back in the day, were long-distance charges.

Whenever Aunt Nerva Jewel would come and visit my grandma and us, she had a long trek home to Lubbock, Texas, over 200 miles. Of course, my mother and grandmother were concerned that she would make it home safe and sound, but how to confirm her arrival without incurring the cost of a long-distance phone call? Enter Mr. Kangaroo!

Once Aunt Nerva Jewel got home, she called the Operator and placed a "collect call to Mr. Kangaroo" at my mom's phone number. Again, I have to interject an explanation, because unless one is of a certain age group, the concept of "calling the Operator" or "placing a collect call" is totally foreign.

Here's how it worked back then:

- If one were calling a local number, that number could simply be dialed.

- However, if one were calling a long-distance number, "0" would be dialed, connecting the caller to a Telephone Company Switchboard Operator. The caller would say, "Please connect me to 555-5555 (or whatever). One could even get information such as telephone numbers and addresses from the Operator. It was the earliest form of Google. The call would be connected, and the long-distance charge would show up on the caller's monthly bill. One could even ask the Operator to notify the caller once three minutes were up, thus saving a little bit of money.

- There was also a way to reverse the charges; the caller would simply ask the Operator to make a "collect call." The Operator would announce the call to the recipient by saying, "So-and-so is calling for so-and-so. Will you accept the charges?" at which point, if the called party would say "Yes," the call would be connected.

So, once my aunt arrived safely at home, she would dial "0" and tell the Operator, "This is Mrs. McAllister. I'd like to make a collect call to Mr. Kangaroo at 123-4567." The Operator would kindly dial my mom and announce the call, "I have a collect call for Mr. Kangaroo. Will you accept the charges?"

When answering the Operator, my mom would say, "I'm sorry, but Mr. Kangaroo isn't here right now." The Operator would relay this information to my aunt, who would say something like, "Thank you, I'll try again later." Thus, my mother and grandmother knew my aunt had arrived home safely.

But where did the idea of "Mr. Kangaroo" even come from? According to my brother, right before my aunt was scheduled to return home from one of her visits, there was a news story on the radio—no television in our home back then—of an escaped kangaroo from a zoo somewhere. Since no one in Southwest Oklahoma or the Texas Plains had any notion of what a kangaroo could do, this announcement instilled terror in all of us. Who could say how dangerous a loose kangaroo could be!?

I think it had to have been my brother, Rodney, who brought sanity back into the conversation, explaining that kangaroos were vegetarians and that it would be no threat. Even with that assurance, my aunt was still very apprehensive as she prepared to leave. Mom reminded her to make a collect call once she got home to let us know she had arrived safely. This time, however, Mom said, "Just make the call to Mr. Kangaroo!" I'm sure my mom was trying to lighten my aunt's fright, and it worked. Thus, Mr. Kangaroo became a part of our family for many years to come; he just wasn't ever available to accept a collect call.

Wet Washcloth Game

Please do not make too harsh a judgment as I explain this next tradition of our family. My own husband and mother-in-law see no humor whatsoever in this "game." I guess one just had to be there to fully appreciate the "Wet Washcloth" game. To clarify, Mom always called this game the "Wet Wash*rag*" game; I referred to it as "wash*cloth*" because I thought it sounded a little more refined … as if such game could ever be classy.

On any given evening, here we would all be, sitting around the living room, watching tv or reading. Again, let me explain that families actually did this once upon a time—they all sat in the same room, *together*, for an extended period of time, almost every evening, *without* cell phones or iPads. Perhaps it was to save electricity costs; only the living room had lights on. Perhaps it was because only one TV was in most households—no iPads, computers, or other entertainment devices were in individual bedrooms. Perhaps it was because people actually talked, shared their day, missed each other, or even liked the company of one's family. Whatever the reason, this was pretty much our family's habit until the early 1970s.

So, back to the living room, where we were all gathered around. One of us, usually my mother, would announce she was getting a Coke or going to the bathroom, so, "please pay attention to the tv, and tell me what I miss." We might hear the refrigerator opening or the toilet flushing—anything to throw us off any suspicion of what was to come.

As she returned, she would casually take her seat, asking, "What'd I miss?" Somehow, we never suspected a thing. This was how good she was at misleading us into a false sense of security.

All of a sudden, *WHAP!* One of us would be smashed upside the head with a damp washcloth, which my mother had thrown with amazing accuracy right into the face of one of her kids. It never hurt, it was never dripping wet, and it was never thrown with force.

There ensued, at least for the next half hour or so, a game of "Wet Washcloth." The recipient would sit quietly, holding the harmless missile, while everyone settled back into their activity. Maybe a minute would pass, maybe several minutes. Then, *WHAP*, the weapon would find a new target.

The "Wet Washcloth" game was not played often, but regularly enough to make it a family tradition, and infrequently enough to always make the element of surprise successful.

I tried to introduce this family game to my husband's kinfolk, specifically his mother, as we were all sitting around watching a boring tv show one evening. No way can I describe exactly how poorly the "Wet Washcloth" game was received, especially on the part of my mother-in-law. Regretfully, this tradition has died a quick death, even though I tried to pass it on to my son for his own family … his wife was also not amused.

So, the only time this damp pastime is revived is when I, my brother, Rodney, and my sister, Jo, are together. It always brings a bunch of laughter and great memories. Outsiders can pooh-pooh all they want; we won't let anyone else rain on our parade … we are already soggy enough.

April Fool's Day

If you haven't already caught on that my mother was a jokester, perhaps this will seal the deal. For most people, April 1st comes and goes with no notice. I believe that April Fool's Day was my mom's favorite holiday. Maybe it was because her birthday was also in April. Regardless, Mom was able to trick us year after year, even into our adulthood. Yes, all of us, kids, might have been a bit gullible; my husband would say I still am.

The joke could be something as simple as running into our bedroom at 3 o'clock in the morning, hollering, "Get up, get up! The alarm didn't go off! You're late for school!" At which point, we would leap out of bed, oblivious to the fact that it was still dark outside, and rush around like crazy, trying to get dressed and gather our books. Right before one of us was awake enough to actually look at a clock, my mother would yell, "April Fools!"

Her pranks were always believable enough to reel us in *every* time. She would never say something like, "Aliens are invading." We would have known it wasn't real if she had made ridiculous statements. No, it was always a very feasible, realistic scenario. Much like today's successful comedians, Mom used very common, everyday events to pull her best hoaxes.

Over the years, it was things like, "The car won't start, you're going to have to walk to school," "It snowed last night, school is canceled," (oh, that one was *cruel)*, or even, "The refrigerator quit; all our food is ruined." The jokes were always reasonable enough to suck us in. And, since it only occurred once a year, we fell for it *every* time.

The trick didn't always occur first thing in the morning. No, Mom was a consummate mischief-maker, knowing exactly the right timing for whatever joke was to be pulled. Maybe it was the middle of the night, "Wake up! Momma [our grandmother] has had a heart attack!" Maybe it was the middle of the day, "Your cousins are on their way to visit; you have to clean your room right now." Maybe it wasn't on all of us kids at the same time, but individually tailored, "Your new dress shrunk in the dryer; you'll have to find something else to wear."

Even as an adult, having moved away and living in my own household, I could expect (but somehow, I never did) a phone call at some point on April Fool's Day. My mom would announce all kinds of calamities from "Your sister is in the hospital" to "I had a car wreck this afternoon." It was years before I got smart enough to start watching the calendar, to be prepared for the joke so I wouldn't die of a stroke before my time. Now, I'm sort of sad that I ever stopped my mother from pulling these gags. It always brought her so much joy to pull one over on us.

Witchcraft and Vampires

Oh, I know what you're thinking now. Surely my mom didn't practice witchcraft! No, she didn't, but she sure loved making my sister and me *think* she had the power to hex us. Even her own sister, my Aunt Nerva Jewel, would sometimes get "cursed" whenever the two of them were arguing. But, to be fair, my aunt would "call upon the angels of God to bring destruction and mayhem" down upon my mother.

To this day, I cannot imagine my saying any such thing to my own sister, or anyone else for that matter. Just demonstrates the drama that we, kids, sometimes had to witness.

My mother *loved* the macabre. She never had time to read a book, but she dearly loved to read the *True Confessions* magazines. She loved vampire stories and scary movies. These little scares were cheap thrills, I guess. The television drama *Dark Shadows* was her all-time favorite tv show. I think my mother actually believed in vampires, werewolves, and other scary beings. She also loved the *Alfred Hitchcock Presents* and *Twilight Zone* series. I learned early to find a book to read while these shows were on. I am a scaredy-cat who has avoided scary movies, haunted houses, and walks in the moonlight all my life. It has never been my choice of entertainment.

I am not exaggerating my avoidance of anything scary. A few years back, because my high school students were all about *Twilight* when those books and movies came out, I decided to read all six books so I'd be aware of what they were talking about. This was really stupid of me ... My home is in the middle of the woods, far from city lights. I found myself locking my car doors when driving home after dark, rushing into our house as fast as I could, heart beating a million miles a minute, imagining vampires coming at me from every direction.

It speaks volumes about my compulsive personality that I continued reading each book despite my frights. Yes, I know that none of this is real. In fact, I'm normally a very logical person. But, put any wild notion into my head, and my vivid imagination can carry me away before logic returns. My mom would have loved the *Twilight* books and movies; it's a shame she passed before vampires came back into vogue.

Just because I've never been into scary stuff doesn't mean I don't like fantasy and sci-fi. I am proud to claim I'm a "Trekkie." And, when *Star Wars* came along, I became just as big a fan. Fast forward to decades later; my 13-year-old grandson referred to Wookies, thinking he was the only one who knew what he was talking about. Imagine his surprise, and the respect I earned, when I responded, "I wonder how he learned how to fly the *Millennium Falcon.*" My own son now has *Star Wars* in common with his young daughter, who aspires to be exactly like Rey.

One of the weirdest things my mother ever did, as far as this side of her personality is concerned, was when I developed a wart on one of my fingers. She convinced me that she could "use her witchcraft skills" to rid me of the unsightly wart. She took me outside after midnight, under the light of a full moon, and rubbed a chicken bone over the wart, mumbling some gibberish that I assume was her version of a spell.

I have no idea if she did this because she actually believed she had powers or if it was some kind of old folk remedy that she was taught as a child. All I know is that the wart actually did drop off within a few weeks. Now before any of my readers think I'm hailing chicken bones at midnight as the latest, greatest wart cure, let me finish. Yes, my wart fell off, but regretfully, it returned within a few years. Warts are caused by a virus, although I didn't know that then. I chose to have it removed by a doctor the next time it appeared.

And, speaking of chicken bones, I should also share with you my mother's belief about a chicken's neck bone. When I was a child, chickens were sold in the grocery stores as a whole chicken. It was plucked, yes, but was sold as a whole bird, much like a small turkey. There were no separately-packaged boneless chicken breasts or drumsticks to be found. In fact, inside every chicken was a packet that contained the "innards" of the chicken—the liver, the heart, the neck, and various other things I'd rather not know about.

Being a frugal housewife, my mom cooked all the above, usually dicing the liver and heart into some sort of gravy (I do not eat gravy to this day), and breading and frying the neck along with the other chicken parts like the thighs, legs, back, and so on. And, because she was trying to make one chicken feed a family of six, she always served the neck to me, saying, "Eat the neck, Dorenda, it'll make you pretty."

Okay, I told you I was gullible. So, yes, I tried my best to gnaw around the neck every time, running to the mirror after dinner to see if it worked. I have to say, especially if one has never attempted to eat a neck bone before, this particular piece of chicken has absolutely NO meat whatsoever. Maybe if I had continued falling for this line, I'd be a lot skinnier than I am today. Alas, I eventually caught on and stopped believing my looks could be transformed by a neck bone.

Reading, 'Riting, and 'Rithmatic

Books have always been my favorite possessions. I learned early on that books take me anywhere I want to go, providing an escape no matter what might be happening around me.

My mother encouraged us to read, not by having a library of hardbound books around, but by gifting us with comic books whenever funds allowed. She, herself, read when she had time, almost always a magazine. As our finances improved over the years, she subscribed to *Reader's Digest* to bring more edifying material into our household. As long as we were reading, we were out of her hair. I guess the comic books were my mother's answer to not having a Tablet or iPad to keep us occupied.

She also encouraged us to write. I've already mentioned her talent for writing poems and songs. As far as I know, only one of my siblings, Taffy, inherited this particular talent. However, I definitely developed a love of the written word, grammar, and creative writing. My favorite assignments in school, besides book reports, were when we were asked to make up a story. Alas, as I grew into an adult, I curtailed my creative streak, putting my writing efforts into lesson plans and business documents.

As for math, my mother thought the only mathematics we needed was that which was required for counting change or paying bills. I believe I've already mentioned that she had an aptitude for doing sums in her head. It is regretful that she had no training or education for finance, such as earning interest on savings, or finding the best interest rate for loans; therefore, none of us, kids, were taught these things, let alone how to balance a checkbook or create a budget. I'm sorry to say that the extent of her teaching us math was to let us count her tips from her waitressing and barmaid jobs.

She never understood why I took algebra or geometry classes in school, even though they were required for my advanced degree. "That's a waste of time; you'll never use that garbage," was a refrain I often heard when I sat down at the kitchen table to do my homework. As an adult, during my short stint as a stockbroker, I never even tried to explain how important it was to invest, put money in savings, or put her money to work for her. All of these concepts were nonsense to a woman who had always lived paycheck to paycheck.

But to say we three kids didn't profit from this would be false. Sometimes, the best lessons are learned as a result of recognizing "what *not* to do."

Christmas

Somehow, someway, my mom always figured out a way to make every Christmas special, in spite of lack of funds. It started with the Sears and Roebuck or J.C. Penney Christmas Toy Catalog arrival in the mail.

We, kids, would pour over every item, reading every description, circling our wishes, and dog-earing the pages. This process didn't take place in one afternoon. Oh, no, it was days and days, and often bled over into our dreams at night ... would that talking Bernie Bernard *really* make me the envy of all the neighborhood kids *and* bring me lifelong happiness? I'm telling you, we, kids, fretted over this bearer of potential Christmas ecstasy more than any world leaders ever worried about peace treaties.

After this catalog was thoroughly digested, we would reluctantly give it to Mom, making sure that she knew *the* item we each wanted most. Sometimes we asked her to return it to us because we had changed our minds. This request was usually ignored by Mom. As a parent and grandparent, I fully understand that now. Had she returned it, our wish list would have continued changing right up until Christmas morning.

No, we didn't get everything we asked for, and in fact, rarely got exactly what we asked for, but Mom always came through for us. Even if she had to find a less expensive substitute for our most-wanted item, we were never disappointed (except for that one Christmas when she forgot to give me anything at all). Looking back, she worked miracles, and I so wish I could tell her now that I finally understand how hard she worked to make Christmas magic for each of us.

One of Mom's traditions was allowing us to open one present on Christmas Eve. I continued this custom with my own son, and he does so with his daughter. Like an appetizer whets the appetite, but at the same time, takes the edge off one's hunger, that one little gift (never the "main" present) lessened the holiday anxiety and allowed each of us, kids, to actually go to sleep with a smile on Christmas Eve.

Movies and Disney

Saying my mother loved the movies would be an understatement. If only she were alive today to have movies on demand with Netflix, that would be awesome. I'm sure that going to a movie at a theater was one of her favorite date activities back in the day.

She loved movies so much that one of my sisters and I were named after movie or tv characters. My name, Dorenda, was the heroine in the 1943 Spencer Tracy movie, *A Guy Named Joe,* although it was actually spelled as "Dorinda." Steven Spielberg remade the movie in 1989 as *Always*, starring Richard Dreyfus and Holly Hunter.

As I remember it, Taffy was the name of a female detective in a tv series in the mid-1960s. However, I was not able to confirm this in my research. The closest thing I could find of a female detective series in the '60s was "*Honey West,*" starring Anne Francis; it was one of the first tv series that showed a strong female character. Who knows if this is what I remember or not, or how my mother got "Taffy" out of "Honey."

As family obligations mounted, going to the movies was a splurge that could not be afforded. I can remember going to only one movie the entire time my mother was married to my father: Disney's *Darby O'Gill and the Little People.* As a kid, I had no notion of the sacrifices my mother made of her own happiness.

Thank goodness for my mother's job as a theater janitor; because of this job, my siblings and I were able to watch all the movies we wanted for several years. To this day, watching a movie is one of my favorite forms of entertainment. I've passed down this pleasure to my grandkids, having "Movie Night" whenever they spend the night, making popcorn the old-fashioned way, on the stove top, turning off the lights, and snuggling on the couch.

Walt Disney's *Wonderful World of Color* was my all-time favorite show on tv, and one that even my mom sat down to watch with us on occasion. To say that Disney had an impact on my life and personality is an underestimation, at best. I wanted to believe in my heart of hearts that *real* life was like Disney movies and shows. I still do.

As a matter of fact, I've done my very best to influence my grandkids accordingly ... I want each of my granddaughters to believe she *is* a princess, albeit one who is a strong, spirited leader who doesn't necessarily need a prince to save her. I want my grandson to model himself after the heroes who have integrity, honesty, courage, and kindness. My step-daughter, Lindsey, is as big a Disney fan as I am and dives feet first into every Disney project I propose. Thank God my husband has helped me perpetuate the Disney attitude by funding numerous Disney World trips, cruises and gifts through the years for each of our seven grandkids.

Horoscopes

My mom was a dedicated believer in astrology and horoscopes. She diligently read hers every single day in the newspaper. Sometimes she read it aloud, but only if it predicted good fortune. She even read ours on occasion. If her horoscope said to avoid going out that day, she would have moved heaven and earth to do so. She believed in it that much. I always believed that horoscopes are self-fulfilling. If you tell yourself something long and loud enough, it will probably happen.

Having been born on April 12th, my mother was an Aries. Whether one believes in such a thing or not, the supposed "inherent traits of the zodiac" definitely seemed to fit my mother's personality. And, as much as my objective side wants to disregard it, my own zodiac sign describes me to a T.

As an Aries, my mother fit the bill of being passionate, exuberant, bold, ambitious, and oftentimes, selfish—putting herself first. She had a cheerful, optimistic disposition, easily leading others because of her own self-confidence. With these traits, it is no wonder she was a terrific salesperson.

According to the zodiac, my own sign, Libra, is a direct opposite to Aries. Whereas Mom was all about "number 1," I have always been more into partnerships and balance. It is no wonder the two of us clashed as often as we did. I wanted harmony and peace; she wanted the next big excitement.

I don't seek out my horoscope as my mother did, but I will read it occasionally for entertainment. I have learned in my lifetime *not* to discount things simply because they seem illogical or because we can't prove they exist. It is this sense of wonder and belief in the impossible that allows me to have faith and optimism in a world that is loaded with disappointments and negatives. I can thank my mother for instilling in me a willingness to believe the impossible *is* possible.

"A Spoonful of Sugar Helps the Medicine Go Down"

Sorry, I couldn't help but quote one of my favorite Disney songs in telling you about this next quirk of my mother's. No matter what our financial status, my mom *always* found a way to sweeten the situation if things were looking or feeling dismal.

No one wants to be sick, and absolutely no kid wants to go to the doctor and get a shot. However, my mother made this childhood necessity into an event that was not only bearable but, to an extent, one of our best memories as kids. Sick? Okay, off to Dr. Allgood's we would go. Unlike today, no appointments were necessary; we would show up in his waiting room, and Dr. Allgood would somehow work us in.

There were two pictures in the waiting room of Dr. Allgood. One was of C. Allen Gilbert's "All is Vanity" painting of a woman admiring herself in a mirror, which looked like death's skull. The other was a cartoonish drawing of a fish with a hook dangling in front of it and the caption, "Even a fish wouldn't get into trouble if it kept its mouth shut."

Looking back, I think these two pictures represented all the wisdom I have ever needed in my life.

But I digress. Once our names were called, Dr. Allgood would take a look in our ears, down our throats, take our temps, and then declare we only needed a penicillin shot. The nurse would come in—she doubled as the receptionist—and give us the needle, always in the behind, never the arm. Once done, we were given a Saf-T-Pop of our own flavor choice. These were the "good" suckers, not like the single stick, flavorless ones of today. However, our sugar fix was just beginning.

As soon as we left Dr. Allgood's, we headed straight for Central Pharmacy. This was one of those old-fashioned drug stores with booths and a counter for the soda fountain. One could order real milkshakes, fountain Cokes, banana splits, cherry limeades, sundaes of all flavors, or even a hamburger. My favorite treat was a chocolate sundae, extra chocolate, with malt sprinkled on top. We were rewarded with the sundae only if we were the kid that got the shot; the other siblings got an ice cream cone. Somehow, knowing this wonderful treat would be coming made all the shots through the years tolerable.

I tried to create the same tradition with my own son, but not having access to an old-fashioned drug store, as well as carrying a guilt trip about feeding my kid so much sugar, this custom kind of died off. What a shame ... Only one of my daughters-in-law, Heather, seems to have picked up where I dropped the ball; she always takes my granddaughters for a treat after a doctor visit. I'm proud she picked up the Sugar Baton.

Love Me, Love My Dog

If such a character trait is genetically passed on, I inherited my mom's love of dogs and animals in *spades*. My grandmother said my mother was exactly like me—she was always bringing home strays. On a farm, having a dog or two was expected. They were part of the workforce, keeping coyotes away from livestock and guarding the family and property. The dog my mom most fondly remembered was her Snowball, a solid white Samoyed or Spitz. I have no idea how she acquired a full-breed dog back then, nor did she ever explain. But, I know she loved that dog more than life itself as she was growing up.

202

We always had a dog once my mother left my dad, and we moved back to Oklahoma. I was constantly bringing home strays. Rusty was my dog for my entire childhood as I was growing up. She was my best friend, my confidant, my solace whenever I needed a shoulder to cry on. She had the softest fur imaginable, a mixed breed with a lot of spaniel. Many dogs won't look you in the eye; Rusty had soulful eyes, and she would always stare straight into mine. When I left home to get married, I didn't take Rusty with me, and I will always regret that. She had to have been about 14 years old at that time.

For a family with no steady source of income, having a pet was a luxury. Although my mother would not allow Rusty to live inside the house, she always made sure my dog had a dog house with warm blankets in the cold months. On those rare occasions when the temps dropped into freezing, she allowed Rusty to stay in the garage. She also made sure Rusty got her rabies shot every year and medical attention when needed.

Once, Rusty almost cut her paw off, attempting to pull a half-opened lid off a tin can. Taking a dog to the vet was the last thing we could afford, yet, my mother made it happen. I think she loved my dog as much as I did.

I learned two things from this event. First and foremost, a pet is a member of the family. They are not disposable and should never be written off because of vet bills or inconvenience. Second, when I open a can with a can opener, I completely remove the lid, never partially opening it enough to dump out the contents.

In her later years, Mom had other dogs, Chows, but by this time in her life, she had relented and started allowing her dogs to stay inside the house with her. This may have been for safety, or it may have been that her heart led her to conclude that dogs are family too.

As for me, I have always believed animals are as important as humans. Don't test me on this, for I won't play the game of whom would I choose to save. I would save *all*.

My son has this same abiding love for animals, and had my mother lived, it would have been something the two of them would have in common. Derrick chose his mate wisely, for Patricia makes sure their four-legged fur babies are well-loved, almost like siblings for my granddaughter. I won't be the least surprised if this particular granddaughter becomes a vet when she grows up. My mother would be proud.

My own occupational leanings did not gravitate toward veterinary care, but that hasn't stopped me from being involved in animal welfare, including being a volunteer zoo docent during summers at one point in my career. I still take in strays—two dogs and a cat at the current time. My husband has banned me from increasing our present load. I try to tell him, I truly don't look for strays … They find ME. Thankfully, I have a vet, Dr. Murphree, who has helped me rescue numerous animals through the years. I pay for the shots and neutering, and he boards them until a home can be found. Every time I save an animal, I feel that I am honoring my mom's memory and love of animals.

Country Music

It was not unusual to get home from school and find that my mother was listening to Loretta Lynn, Tammy Wynette, Johnny Cash, Patsy Cline, or Jim Reeves, to name a few. It isn't a hard stretch to compare my mother's life to the lyrics of many of the songs. It's partially why I chose to entitle each chapter of this book with a country song.

If my mother sang along with the songs, I don't recall ever hearing her. I think she believed her own voice was poor, or that she couldn't carry a tune. All four recordings of her songs, which I still have, were sung by others, not my mother. What a treasure it would be to have her voice recorded, no matter how off-key, singing the lyrics she created.

Singing is a joyful act, and one that I engage in almost daily. I'm not saying I have a wonderful voice—I don't, but I love to sing or hum along with my favorite songs. God love my husband … He's never once complained about my lack of singing talent. Whether I'm in the car by myself, in the shower, or cleaning the house, I'll belt out a tune or two. It's uplifting and brings a smile to my face.

I've tried to teach my grandkids the same, as well as teaching my son to sing when he was growing up. I hope some of his favorite memories are of our sitting with a Disney songbook, learning new songs. He could sing the Pinocchio song, "I've Got No Strings," and the "Supercalifragilisticexpialidocious" song before he was 4 years old. One of my granddaughters, at age 3, loves to sing at the top of her lungs, "Pharaoh, Pharaoh" by Billy Jonas; Loxley brings joy to all who hear her.

Thanks to my mother, I love music. Her musical preference was country music. Mine is very eclectic. I wish I had the talent to read notes or play an instrument, but alas, I have to content myself with listening and singing along.

Lessons Learned

Overall, I believe I learned from Mom that one does not need a lot of money or things to be happy, or to be playful. I also learned:

- It is quite possible to bring laughter to others, as well as oneself, with simple actions, stories, and unique traditions.

- Never take myself too seriously.

- Look for joy wherever possible, be it in a daily horoscope, song, favorite tv show or movie, book, my dog, or even getting a shot at the doctor so I could justify getting an ice cream sundae.

- Choose a mate with a light heart and a willingness to play, tease, and laugh—it will keep us young forever. (Thank you, Jimmy.)

I hope I have taught my son and all my grandkids to do the same.

This chapter was one of the easiest for me to write, as I combed my memories and asked my siblings for their best stories. As I was writing it, I would literally wake myself up sometimes, laughing out loud, as a particular recollection would make its way into my self-consciousness.

Not so with this next chapter. I'll prepare you now ... the following section is not for the faint-hearted. In fact, it was the hardest chapter of this entire book for me to write. I've made it as short as possible and still do justice to my mother's story. Take heart; it's not the end of her tale. I refuse to end on a downer note.

Chapter 9

The Downfall

This is my shortest chapter because it was very painful for me to write. You will think me the most selfish, most horrible of daughters when you finish reading this chapter. I am guilty as charged. My only defense is that I was hundreds of miles away, but the reality is that I could have been next door, and it would have made no difference. I had chosen to separate my own and my immediate family's life from the existence of my mother's. This choice was made not because I didn't love my mom. It was made because I loved my son and husband more.

The downfall started when my youngest sister, Taffy, was in junior high school in the late 1970s. I had been married for several years, finished college, and was teaching in Lawton, Oklahoma, where my husband and I lived, about an hour from Altus. My brother, Rodney, was married and lived at least three hours away. My sister, Jo, had graduated from high school and was working in OKC, again, at least three hours away.

I talked, by phone, to my mother every few weeks, but honestly was too busy with my own life to be involved with hers. She was finally settled with a good man who made a decent wage, didn't drink, and they lived in a house that was their own. Buck had even adopted my sister, Taffy (whose dad was husband #6). Mom still worked, selling insurance and real estate, but it was because she wanted her own spending money, not because she had to put a roof over their heads or food on the table. To say I was out of touch with what was going on with my mom is an understatement.

I was at work when I was summoned to the office for an emergency phone call from my mother.

"Taffy has been arrested for drugs. She was framed. Some girls at school did it." I immediately took off work to head to Altus, thinking the entire time, this cannot be true. Not my little sister. Spoiled, yes. At age 13, already an obnoxious teenager, but still, Taffy was merely a little kid. When I arrived at my mom's house, she was beside herself, screaming at Buck, blaming everyone but Taffy. I told her I would go to the school to see what I could find out.

At Northeast Junior High School, my old alma mater, I learned that my innocent little sister was *not* guilt-free, not at all. It wasn't the first time she had been caught with drugs. It wasn't the first time she had been involved in a fight on school grounds. However, it was the first time that DHS (Department of Human Services) got involved and had taken my sister into juvenile custody.

When I returned to my mother's house, I confronted her with these facts. She tried to deny everything but ultimately confessed to knowing all these things were true. Still, she blamed Taffy's friends and even Buck's sons, who didn't even live with them. I scoffed at this, knowing that it was no one's fault but my sister's. It was years later that I learned that one of Buck's sons *may* have had drug addictions and juvenile convictions. Whether they started my little sister on drugs or not really doesn't matter; the damage was done.

From that incident, a downward spiral began. My sister stole the family car and drove it through someone's house. She was arrested, placed in juvenile custody, and released time and again. I can't count the number of times, or the amount of money Mother and Buck spent on rehab facilities for my sister, Taffy. At age 20, she got pregnant by another loser druggie; my mother and Buck forced a wedding so that my niece would have a legitimate birth. The marriage lasted only a few months, as far as I know. When my niece was 10, Mom and Buck officially took temporary custody of her because my sister was still doing and dealing drugs.

None of us had any idea how bad things were in Mom's household. She never told any of us how horrible life had become. Many years later, I found a letter or journal entry my mother wrote, front and back, on spiral notebook paper. It describes a nightmare, an intolerable existence for every person in that house ... literally, physical and mental abuse being perpetrated against my elderly mother. It also makes me realize that Mom was losing her coherence; her mind was definitely affected by all the turmoil.

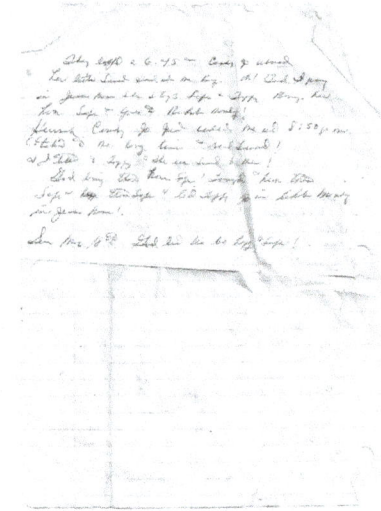

Translation: What would I steal from my Baby? All I want to do in life is take care of Taffy & Candy Jo! She kept her hand over my mouth & I don't know what to do. She asked Candy Jo for a Pillow to put over my face & smother me! & Candy Jo did it! Oh! God how could my Grandbaby do this to her NaNa? I always thought she would take up for me & at least scream but she told Taffy to knock me in the head. I don't know if I will forgive this or not. Buck finally got his A home & they let me out & Candy Jo blocked the door & I didn't want to hurt her so I kept asking for Taffy to let me out & she said C.J. let her out & finally she did but she shoved me down into the cedar chest & I Slapped Leg! She cried. I apologized to her. I love my child & grandchild so & wonder where I went so wrong? I am so scared of her because she is on dope so bad she don't know what she's doing! I should kick her out but it will ruin her life & Candy Jo's life! I went to Kelly's to get my hair combed & took Taffy and C.J. with me & Taffy had her hair tinted & oh! God she's so mean to me & took her to stranger's house. Don McDonald? I pray they will be home safe! Buck filled up her pick up & put new tags on! (over)

They left at 6:45 & Candy Jo waved her little sweet hand at me By. Oh! God I pray in Jesus name she stays safe & Taffy brings her home safe & goes to Rehab Monday! Hurrah Candy Jo just called me at 8:50 pm & talked to me long time & real sweet! & I talked to Taffy & she was sweet to me! God bring them home safe! Tonight & keep them safe and keep them safe & let Taffy go in Rehab Monday in Jesus name!

Sun Mar 18th. God let us be happy & Safe!

Figure 66 Journal page from my mother.

Mom's Journal Page

What would I steal from my Baby? All I want to do in life is take care of Taffy & Candy Jo! She kept her hand over my mouth & I don't know what to do. She asked Candy Jo for a Pillow to put over my face & smother me! & Candy Jo did it! Oh! God how could my Grandbaby do this to her NaNa? I always thought she would take up for me & at least scream but she told Taffy to knock me in the head. I don't know if I will forgive this or not. Buck finally got his A home & they let me out & Candy Jo blocked the door & I didn't want to hurt her so I kept asking for Taffy to let her out & she said C.J. let her out & finally she did but she shoved me down into the cedar chest & I slapped Leg! She cried. I apologized to her. I love my child & grandchild so & wonder where I went so wrong? I am so scared of her because she is on dope so bad she don't know what she's doing! I should kick her out but it will ruin her life & Candy Jo's life! I went to Kelly's to get my hair combed & took Taffy and C.J. with me & Taffy had her hair tinted & oh! God she's so mean to me & took her to stranger's house. Don McDonald? I pray they will be home safe! Buck filled up her pick up & put new tags on! (over)

They left at 6:45 & Candy Jo waved her little sweet hand at me By. [sic] Oh! God I pray in Jesus name she stays safe & Taffy brings her home safe & goes to Rehab Monday! Hurrah Candy Jo just called me at 8:50 pm & talked to me long time & real sweet! & I talked to Taffy & she was sweet to me! God bring them home safe! Tonight & keep them safe and keep them safe & let Taffy go in Rehab Monday in Jesus name!

Sun Mar 18th. God let us be happy & safe!

All of this took a financial toll on Mom and Buck, not to mention a terrible toll on their health; they both would have been in their 70s by this point. Because Altus is such a small town, their reputations were ruined. Mom persuaded Buck that they could all have a fresh start by moving to OKC. She was also convinced that by moving Taffy and my niece away from Altus, they would end their drug connections. Regretfully, drug connections exist everywhere.

I have been told that, in exchange for drugs, my sister, Taffy, pimped out my niece, her own daughter, by the time she turned 14. I do not know if this is true, but I do know that both my sister and niece were heavy into drugs and all the crimes associated with them by the early 2000s. Each of

213

their rap sheets describes "possession of controlled substance," "distribution of controlled substance," "forgery," "assault and battery with a deadly weapon," "shooting with intent to kill," and "maintaining a place for keeping/selling controlled substance." It was this last charge that spelled the beginning of the end for my mother and Buck.

Because their home in OKC was implicated in the charge and drug raid, both were arrested, along with my sister, Taffy, and my niece. I was living in a different state, so I did not hear the news that night, but my poor sister, Jo, and my brother, Rodney, heard about "the notorious Buchanan Gang" having been apprehended after a police chase.

Mom and Buck were released the next morning, but not until Buck spent their very last dime on a defense attorney. They lost their home and every possession they owned. They moved back to Altus. A run-down rent house would be the last home Buck lived in before his death in 2008. He died penniless, with only his Masonic friends and fellow veterans to honor him.

Still, my mom would not give up on my sister or niece. She continued supporting them, sending every cent she had to their respective prisons, even doing without food or medicine for herself. She was too proud to ask for anything from my siblings or me. We were too helpless to make her see that she was only enabling both her youngest daughter and her granddaughter to continue their drug habits.

When my sister, Taffy, was finally released in 2010, my mother moved back to OKC, renting a small but clean house in an older section of the city. My brother, Rodney, my sister, Jo, and I banded together to try and help them both get a fresh start. Because I was several states away, my contribution was in the form of funding, while my sister and brother did all the leg work of taking my newly-released sister to required counseling, meetings with probation officers, job interviews, and doctor and dentist visits. Years on drugs and being in the prison system had resulted in my beautiful sister having no teeth left.

It is ironic, if not counter-productive, that the legal system, which imprisoned my sister for drug abuse, created even further drug addiction for her by requiring her to take a drug that "kept her calm" during her entire incarceration. We also learned that my sister would be required to "pay back" all financial damages once she was released. She owed the state of Oklahoma a ridiculous amount of money in restitution. She was behind the eight-ball and had no way of gaining ground without a job. And, it was near impossible to get a job because she was a convicted felon.

Although it wasn't the best environment—Mom and Taffy argued constantly—it was at least a roof over their heads, food in their bellies, and hope that things would soon improve once Taffy got a job. We *all* had hope because it seemed that my sister, Taffy, had finally learned her lesson and was determined to turn her life around.

Things went horribly wrong, however, when my niece was also released from prison within the year. I'm not at all sure what happened, who was at fault, but the house of cards crumbled almost overnight. My sister and my niece were back on drugs, and my mother was thrown out of the rent house, again losing all her possessions.

I received a phone call from my sister, Taffy, sobbing and telling me she had no place to go, that Mom had thrown her out. I wired money to her so she could get a hotel room; in hindsight, I'm pretty sure she used the money for a high. After that, I didn't hear from her again for several months.

Meanwhile, my siblings and I completely lost contact with my mother and niece. Mom wouldn't even call any of us. It was by the grace of God that my brother, Rodney, found out where Mom and my niece were living. Rodney does a lot of charity work for various churches, including taking and serving meals at different locations for the homeless. Through his connections, he was able to get a possible address for my mother. This all took place around Thanksgiving in 2011. My siblings and I decided to go to the address to check on Mom.

Oh my God, the place was a hovel. Drugs and thugs were everywhere. I was physically sick to see what my mother had sunk to. Cardboard only on the windows, no glass. No electricity. No refrigerator. Mother was a hollow shell of herself, dirty, with no way to bathe. She refused to come with us because "Candy will be right back. I can't leave her."

We all knew our niece was still dealing, and possibly worse, but we could not convince Mom to abandon her. My siblings and I went to buy groceries for Mom, but it had to be things she could keep in her little ice chest, nothing perishable. By the time we had returned with the groceries, my niece had shown up with what had to have been her pimp. It was November, cold, but my niece had *no shoes* on her feet. She was probably high as a kite.

I can only tell you that I *tried* my best to talk my mother into leaving with us. I promised she could either live with me, or I would buy her a trailer of her own, *if* she would come back with me to Alabama. My conditions were that she leave immediately ... *and* she had to break all ties with my

216

niece and sister. She would not agree to this. I knew I could not bring all that trouble home to my own family or grandchildren. So, we, three, left my mother sitting in a rickety lawn chair inside a house with no heat or utilities. It has to be one of the hardest things any of us has ever done, to leave my mother in that dump.

We called Adult Protective Services that night; it was obvious to us that my niece and her cohorts were taking my mother's Social Security checks, barely keeping her alive. Things came to a head almost immediately; my niece landed back in prison, and my mother ended up relocating to Altus again. She was once again in a rent house, only this time, it was a "rent-to-own" monstrosity. But at least she was making a life for herself again without the leaches of my sister, my niece, and their druggie lowlifes.

Lowlifes, however, come in all makes and models, we soon learned. The "rent-to-own" scenario is nothing more than a scam on poor or uneducated people who can't qualify for a legitimate home loan. The elderly are especially susceptible to these rip-offs. The payments are more than what typical rent would be, and yet, the realty office carrying the note is *not* responsible for any repairs because, "Hey, you're buying this home; you're responsible for anything that goes wrong."

Figure 67 Mother in her last home ... the "rent-to-own" monstrosity.

Even more lowlifes came out of the woodwork once the neighborhood gossip mill disclosed there was new "prey" in town. Mother was targeted as "the old lady who needed things"—the lawn mowed, a ride to the grocery store or doctor, minor repairs, anything that would give the scammer an excuse to go to my mom's door and offer said services.

"That'll be $20, Jo; gas is really expensive, and my car uses at least that much to go the one mile to the store." "Sure, I can get you a used window AC unit, but it's going to cost at least $500, Jo, but that's a real bargain 'cause new ones cost $5000." They all had Mom convinced they were doing her favors. She was sure all these lowlifes were her friends.

My mother was too proud to let any of us know about all the swindles being pulled on her. Meanwhile, her Social Security check was being drained by these shysters as well as by my sister and niece. How, you might ask, since both Taffy and her daughter were imprisoned?

218

Well, both incarcerated relatives stayed in touch with Mom, constantly asking for money to be sent so "the mean girl in the next cell won't beat me up," or "so I can bribe the guard not to rape me," or "so I can get a candy bar for my birthday—they are $10 in here," or "so I can buy an interview outfit for when I get released." The excuses were endless, and so were the financial demands on Mom.

Although all three of us siblings maintained closer contact with Mom than we had before, we assumed things were okay since both my sister and niece were back in prison. We were all very naïve in respect to how corrupt the penal system is. I am not saying that every prison employee is "on the take," but there are more than a few that consistently break rules for their own gain. The biggest users and abusers in the prison system, however, are the inmates.

After all the horrible stories of prison life that we have seen in the movies over the years, I now believe there is at least a grain of truth in each and every one of them. My siblings and I are firmly convinced that a truly sorrowful, remorseful, or reformed prisoner is a rare being indeed. Instead, we would argue that most criminals become even worse once incarcerated, and any remorse over their crimes that they might show is simply that ... *Show* so that they can pull their next scam.

Since I've never been incarcerated myself, you might wonder how I can make these statements with any validity. I make these observations based on actual letters my mother received from various inmates who were supposed "friends" of Taffy or Candy at their respective institutions. Mom was targeted as an easy mark, an old lady with Social Security money. Why not bribe or threaten her into sending money all the time?

Several years ago, the Oklahoma Prison System instituted a payment system called JPay. No cash is allowed to be sent directly to any prisoner. Instead, the donor must send money electronically to the prisoner's account "for a fee." So instead of my mom losing only a $20 bill to an inmate's scam, it actually cost her at least an additional $5 to $12 for each and every transaction.

I used to lecture my students, as well as my son, to never complain about something if one didn't have some constructive solutions in mind. The prison system is broken, and I don't have solutions. The problems start with many of the attorneys; I'm sorry to say. The news is full of people who get away with crimes every day, solely because they had the financial means to get a better lawyer. I wish with all my heart that I had solutions to these problems.

We might never have been aware of these slime balls preying on Mom except for the fact that my mother suffered "extreme aortic stenosis" and ended up in the hospital in Altus in late 2012. Her weight had dropped below 90 lbs; Mom was about 5'5" and always maintained a weight of 140 lbs, so she had dropped a third of her normal size.

I flew to Oklahoma immediately because I was the only one of my siblings who could take time off from work. It was obvious that Mom needed long-term rehabilitation. There didn't seem to be a good option for that kind of care in Altus, so we had her transferred to a long-term care facility in OKC, not far from either of my siblings. The doctor specifically said, "She cannot ever go back home to Altus; she needs 24-hour care right now, and if the therapy works, she *has* to live close to family here in Oklahoma City so that someone can check on her every day."

Once again, we three siblings joined forces to try and make Mom's life easier. My brother, Rodney, visited her several times a day, bringing her treats from Starbucks, and praying with her, while my sister, Jo, and I traveled back to Altus to tie up loose ends.

Those loose ends were VERY tangled—loan shark cards taped to my mother's front door, unpaid bill notices in the mail, threats of foreclosure from various and sundry businesses. It took about three days for us to contact all legitimate entities, settle payments, and close accounts.

The other things we found told us more than we would have ever heard out of Mom's mouth. She had unfilled prescriptions, no food in the house, Taffy's pickup in the driveway—not drivable, but still, Mom was keeping payments and insurance current on it for my sister's sake. We found checkbook registers where the only expenses were checks paid to Taffy and my niece, wiping out her only income, her Social Security, every single month. I'm sure that if we had compared my mom's phone record with the checkbook, we would have found the calls from my sister and niece synchronized with the money withdrawals. It was clear as day that Mom had stopped caring for herself so that she could have more money to give to Taffy and my niece.

While we were in Altus, Jo and I went through my mom's house, saving what we could but choosing to let most of the cheap furnishings be repossessed with the "rent-to-own" house. It was during this cleansing that we found the extortion letters from complete strangers, inmates, and even our own niece. By this time, our sister, Taffy, was once again out of prison, supposedly being transferred to a halfway house in the OKC area.

I sent my sister, Taffy, a heart-rending letter detailing Mom's deteriorated health, telling her what the doctor said. I *begged* her to use her influence to convince Mom to stay in OKC, to *not* return to Altus. I encouraged her to make the halfway house thing work, find a job, and stand on her own two feet so that there would be four of us helping Mom for a change. Honestly, I don't remember if I heard back from Taffy. Ultimately, she joined up with a biker guy and ended up in Arizona for the next few years.

Meanwhile, between the three of us and the rehab center, we took care of Mom, ensuring that she was gaining strength and mobility, being well-fed, and taking required medications. During the worst of her illness, I had taken over her checking account, monitoring all expenses and paying all bills. As she gained her health, she asked that she get her checkbook back so she could, once again, begin doing it herself. I had no problem giving it back because I knew her pride had suffered greatly when she was helpless for so many months. This turned out to be my greatest mistake.

The three of us constantly talked to Mom about OKC living options once she was released, encouraging her to do everything the doctors asked so she could get out as soon as possible. We had checked into senior housing in the OKC area and offered her the alternative of moving to Alabama to live with me. She continued to state her wishes to return to Altus, but we continued to state emphatically that this was *not* possible. I did not realize at the time that my mother was no longer capable of rational thinking; she had it in her head that she must return to Altus in order to provide for Taffy and my niece whenever they got out of prison. She was coherent enough, though, to convince my siblings and me that she had learned her lesson.

We were regularly assured by not only Mom but the rehab staff that she had no contact with my sister or my niece. This was a falsehood.

Mother had a friend named Linda who was as much an enabler as Mom had ever been. She passed information between my niece and Mom, making plans to return my mother to Altus as soon as the doctors released her. This was the reason Mom wanted control of her checkbook again; she wanted to have money ready to make payments for that horrible rent-to-own house again.

In fairness to Linda, she saw my siblings and me as interfering outsiders who had no business taking over my mother's life and finances; Linda was also being manipulated by my niece as well. So when my niece was once again released from prison, she knew exactly where to find Mom, thanks to Linda, and immediately went to the rehab center to confront my mother.

We will never know exactly what transpired that day, October 5th, 2015. However, the facts are that my niece arrived at the facility that evening with a male friend and went straight to Mom's room. She obtained a check from my mother in the amount of Mom's entire checkbook balance. Mother's Social Security check had been direct-deposited the day before, and because of years of experience, both Taffy and Candy Jo knew full well what date funds would be available each month.

Mom had signed the check, and it was cashed that evening. By 8:07 a.m. on October 6th, the next morning, my

223

mother was dead upon arrival at the hospital, having suffered a massive heart attack.

I will always be convinced that my niece caused Mom's heart failure; at least two of the staff members of the rehab center told me, as we went to pick up Mom's belongings, that "An altercation occurred, and your niece and her friend had to be removed from the facility by security."

The lady who resided in the room next to Mom said, "That trashy girl was screaming horrible things at your mom, cussing her, threatening her, and telling her they would kill her if she didn't hand over her money."

The fault lies at my own door as well. If I had not returned my mother's checkbook, there would have been no money to extort. If I could have predicted my niece's showing up, perhaps I could have prevented the altercation that evidently sent my mother over the edge. If Linda had not informed my niece that Mother, once again, had control of her finances, maybe my niece would never have bothered to go see her grandmother. A lot of what-ifs, which accomplish nothing.

Every time I read this chapter, I feel like I'm having an anxiety attack—short of breath, stomach clenching, headache pounding. I apologize, for airing our dirty secrets, but it was a part of my mother's last days. I had to tell it.

Brighter days are ahead in the next chapter.

Chapter 10

NOT the Worst Mother After All

"Best of My Love" by The Eagles

October 6th, 2015, I was notified my mother had suddenly died of a heart attack. I wasn't there. I didn't get a chance to tell her one more time that I loved her. And I most certainly didn't get the opportunity to make her feel that I valued her ... because at that time, regretfully, I did not.

Although I am the middle child, somehow, I was chosen by my siblings to deliver the eulogy and plan my mother's memorial. I remember thinking it should be my older brother or either of my two younger sisters—anyone but me because I had always had the most troubled relationship with my mom.

The cliché "God works in mysterious ways" seems to have held true, though, because it seems that I was the right person for the job. It is my personality to be detail-oriented, seek facts, and try and put a positive spin on whatever facts I find.

So, as my siblings and I dug through the debris of my mom's 87-year life to prepare for her memorial service, we discovered a *much better* person than we had ever credited her to be. Of course, my siblings and I knew bits and pieces of her history; we *thought* we knew her. However, in the aftermath of her death, many, many wonderful things came to light. I had barely scratched the surface of these details when I prepared her eulogy. I knew I wanted her eulogy to focus on the positives of her life and be uplifting to those in attendance at her memorial.

I ended up using a poem on the memorial program that my sister, Taffy, had written for Mom years before. It is entitled, "Catch Me When I Fall." I still cannot read it without crying. It totally captures the relationship my mother had with my sister … With all of us, really.

There were too many aspects of her existence, though, that weren't appropriate to be shared in the memorial. Some were good, some not so much. The idea of writing this book took root in my brain over five years ago and wouldn't let go. Once I retired, I knew the time had come for me to share with the world the story of this complicated woman who was my mother.

Once I started writing, there were nights when I couldn't sleep, when I had nightmares because of unearthing unpleasant memories that I had buried for years. I could fully relate when my sister, Jo, asked me to stop discussing the book with her, that it was too painful for her to think about. My brother, Rodney, continued to be supportive and helpful with his own memories; he seems to have reached a much better level of acceptance of my mother than have I or Jo. Even my sister-in-law, Terri, shed light on incidents and memories from a different perspective. Turns out, we *all* thought we were raising Mom, that we *all* loved but didn't particularly *like* her.

My mother was a very complex person, and there will always be a part of her that I **do not** like. But now, after learning so much about Mom and allowing time to put things into perspective, as well as gaining a little maturity, I can **accept** those aspects of my mother. And, I've learned that there are many, many more parts of her that I do indeed like, admire, and aspire to emulate.

The writing of this book has been cathartic for me. I have ridden a roller coaster of emotions ... sad ones like sorrow, guilt, regret, empathy, distress, and even anger or resentment. But I also felt happy ones like surprise, pride, admiration, love, understanding, and ultimately, a loyalty to this woman that I had never experienced before in my life. Maybe all these emotions are part of the grief process.

I know that for the first time in my life, I can actually relate to my mother. I feel that I now understand her decisions, I am no longer angry at her, I forgive her mistakes, I actually *like* and admire the woman she was despite all her faults. Who am I to judge her? Last time I looked, I think my house is made of glass too.

I've also found that I can let go of self-disgust; it no longer bothers me when I think, say or do something that reminds me of my mother. I am finally healing.

Most importantly, I no longer think she was the *worst mother ever (which was one of my original titles for this book).*

Mom never gave us up for adoption, even though it would have made her life simpler. She always put a roof over our heads and food in our bellies, even though she had to sacrifice her own dignity to do so. Mom always loved and accepted us, no matter how distant, arrogant, self-righteous, or selfish we became.

Did she make mistakes? Yes. Was she a bad person? *No.* The only thing she was truly guilty of was the nonjudgmental love and unconditional forgiveness that I have hammered on throughout this book. It is regrettable that certain individuals took advantage of this.

These are the final lessons my mother has taught me, even after her death ...

- Give *nonjudgmental love* to your parents, siblings, significant others, and even your friends *before* it is too late.

- *Unconditionally forgive* others for their mistakes; holding grudges only destroys the best part of ourselves.

- Even if you can't fully understand why a person makes the decisions they do, acknowledge that this is their right, their free will, and as long as it doesn't affect you or yours directly, learn to *accept* the person for who they are.

- No matter your religious leanings, perhaps there is some form of the Ten Commandments: I have learned the hard way that it is *very* important to *always*, "*Honor* thy mother and father." Love and accept them as human beings—faults, imperfections, and all. By doing so, we learn to accept and love ourselves.

I sincerely want others to learn from my mistakes before it's too late. Pick up the phone. Call your parent(s) or sibling(s), or whoever it is that you have been holding at arm's length. Tell her (or him) about the *love* you feel. Better yet, go say this in person.

One more section, the Epilogue. Welcome to Mom's memorial service.

Epilogue

My Mother's Memorial Service

"I Don't Need No Rockin' Chair" by Merle Haggard

Catch Me When I Fall

You're with me through it all,

You catch me when I fall . . .

Through the good times and the bad,

You never get angry or mad.

You're always with me until the end,

Your word will never break nor bend . . .

And over every mountain tall,

There's no sin too big or too small,

You can knock down any wall,

You always catch me when I fall!

Written by:
Taffy Buchanan
(Daughter)
1/11/2005

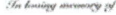

In loving memory of
Sadie Jo (Lowry) Buchanan
April 12, 1928 - October 6, 2015

In Loving Memory of

Sadie Jo (Lowry) Buchanan

April 12, 1928 to October 6, 2015

Sadie Jo (Lowry) Buchanan, age 87, passed away October 6, 2015, in Oklahoma City, OK. She was born in Hollis, OK on April 12, 1928, the youngest of nine children. She was a member of Emmanuel Baptist Church of Altus, OK. She is proceeded in death by her husband, Harold Buck Buchanan, her parents, Minerva & Samuel Lowry, and her brothers and sisters, Cecil, Dollie Weightman, Loy, Ray, Hubert, and Dewey Lowry. Sadie Jo has two surviving sisters—Fay Gatlin of TN and Nerva Jewel Sherman of TX, as well as several nieces and nephews. Four children and their spouses and two stepsons also survive her—Rodney Brown (wife Terri) of Edmond, OK, Dorenda Doyle (husband Jimmy) of Cullman, AL, Alonzo Issend/Vo Wisorld (Bit, AZ, Me Bux), Taffy Lambert (husband Russell) of Wickenburg, AZ, Mike Buchanan of Norman, OK, and Gary Buchanan of Huntley, IL.

Sadie Jo has five surviving grandchildren—Natalie Bingham of Noble, OK, Rev. Matthew Brown (wife Bonnie) of Ft. Gibson, OK, Dr. Derrick Taff (wife Patricia) of State College, PA, ?Alcharia of Uplt. ?. o. rriol as dias.gr?k? OKC, OK, and Candice Buchanan of OKC. OK, as well as one step-grandson, Toby Whiteside of OKC, OK.

Sadie Jo was blessed with seven great-grandchildren—Jorden Brown, Samuel Brown, Elliana Brown, Tyler Bingham, Dustin Staats, Becky Staats, and Appleton Taff.

Sadie Jo Buchanan was known as a superior salesperson, having made a living selling real estate, insurance, and encyclopedias at various times in her life. Memorial Services will be held at Emmanuel Baptist Church in Altus, OK on November 14, 2015 at 10 am. In lieu of flowers, the family suggests donations to Emmanuel Baptist Church of Altus, OK in honor of Sadie Jo Buchanan.

Memorial Services for
Sadie Jo (Lowry) Buchanan
November 14, 2015
Emmanuel Baptist Church
Altus, OK

Order of Service

Opening Prayer . . . . Rev. Boyd Whitehead
Pastor of Emmanuel Baptist Church, Altus, OK

"Amazing Grace" . . . . Congregation

Tributes to Sadie Jo Buchanan . . . . Read by Dorenda Doyle,
Rodney Brown for Dr. Derrick Taff (grandson),
for Fay Gatlin (sister)

Eulogy . . . . Rev. Boyd Whitehead

"I Can Only Imagine" . . . . Rev. Matthew Brown
Pastor of Calvary Faith Church, Ft. Gibson, OK
(grandson)

Benediction (Closing Prayer) . . . . Rev. Boyd Whitehead

Amazing Grace

Amazing grace! How sweet the sound
That saved a wretch like me!
I once was lost, but now am found;
Was blind, but now I see.

Through many dangers, toils and snares,
I have already come;
'Tis grace hath brought me safe thus far,
And grace will lead me home.

When we've been there ten thousand years,
Bright shining as the sun,
We've no less days to sing God's praise
Than when we'd first begun.

Tribute to My Mom, Jo Buchanan

By Dorenda Doyle

Our mother was known to most of you as just "Jo." And there could never be more of a misnomer because Mom was *anything but* your "average Joe." In fact, I think most of you will agree that our "Jo" was one of a kind.

On the "outside," Mom was always well-dressed (my brother-in-law pointed out that she "always had a suit on"), well-made-up, with her hair always in place. She was considered a *beautiful woman* from the time she was a child until very recent years. She always wore Avon's Occur perfume or White Diamonds. And, she *always* wore a *smile.*

I am my mom's second child, her oldest daughter, the middle kid, and the one she most consistently considered her "problem child." *Not* for the usual reasons, but because I had a smart-aleck attitude, and I don't think she ever knew how to deal with that.

Rodney, our big brother, was Mom's first child, her only boy, and was always near-perfect in Mom's eyes because of this. Jo, my little sister, was always Mom's "sweetest and prettiest child." Rodney and I would agree with Mom's estimation, because Jo still pretty much is the sweetest one of any of Mom's kids. Taffy is our youngest sister, but couldn't be here today, and I think all of us would agree, was Mom's "favorite," probably because she came along late in Mom's life and was the baby of the family.

I want to tell you today about "Jo"—our mother ... what she *was* to us ... what she *did* for us ... what she *gave* to each of us.

What She WAS to Us

Mom was never the traditional mother of the 1950s or '60s. In other words, she wasn't a "stay-at-home" mom, watching soap operas, wearing pearls, joining the PTA, etc.

No, *our mother* was, at various times during our growing-up years, a *single* mother, self-supporting, self-educated, extremely *hard-working* mother who *always* kept a roof over our heads and food on the table. At times, I can remember her holding at least three jobs simultaneously, mostly sales. If I had to use *one word* to describe my mom, I would use *"optimistic."* No matter what tragedies befell her, she *always* focused on the silver lining of the dark cloud hanging over her head. She *always* instilled in each of us a "pull-yourself-up-by-your-bootstraps" attitude. I cannot remember her *ever* having the old "woe is me" ... "life is so cruel" ... or even, "Why is this happening to *me*?" attitude.

Instead, she instilled in *each* of us a *"never give up,"* "solve the problem" attitude. For that, Mom, I will *always* be grateful.

What She DID for Us

Mom, through the years, gave us such memories as the "Wet Washrag" game, unforgettable April Fool's jokes (she *never* gave up trying to fool us each year), Mr. Kangaroo, or even dressing us alike (only me and Jo, not you, Rodney). We all have fond memories of her taking us for ice cream sundaes at Central Pharmacy after a shot at Dr. Allgood's.

Mom was at times very lucky but somehow always missed out on the "big strike" that might have made a huge difference in her life. As you look at pictures of her in the back of this sanctuary, you might notice that Mom cut a few records—these were demos of songs she had written (not sung), some extremely good!

She was literally in negotiations with Patsy Cline's management in the early 1960s when that singer met her tragic death ... Mom's hopes and dreams of becoming a songwriter going down in flames, just as surely as that star's plane did.

That's, regretfully, how it was in the '50s and '60s for women—no support group or resources to allow them to follow dreams or to reward talents because women were expected to fit the "Susie Homemaker" mold.

I am fully aware of what Mom gave up in terms of her own career, fame, and fortune, basically so that she could raise and support the four of us kids. She NEVER gave us up or gave up on us. She NEVER allowed us to go on welfare. And despite our growing up in trailer parks with her working most nights as a barmaid or waitress, or cleaning theaters or hotels as a janitor, she NEVER allowed any of us to act like or to consider ourselves "white trash" just because of our economic circumstances.

As most of you are aware, Mom changed husbands about as often as she changed wigs ... and she outlasted them ALL—husbands AND wigs!

For all that, I believe each of you will agree that our mom was an extremely outgoing, friendly person, and as one of my cousins put it, "a woman with the BIGGEST HEART who would give the shirt off her back to most anyone." She GENUINELY CARED about the people she knew and did business with.

What She GAVE to Us

And with that, I want to point out the *most wonderful gifts* our mother gave to each of us ...

Rodney, you got Mom's work ethic—in *spades*! You will *always* give 200 percent to every job you ever have, not because it pays well or deserves your hard work or loyalty, but because it's the *right* thing to do; you'll always show up early and work late, never calling in sick. This is evident in your 35-year career with the phone company. It's what Mom demonstrated to us all our lives. She was *so* proud of the man you are—a good and faithful husband, father, and provider, certainly, but mostly, the devout *Christian* you are. She trusted your prayers more than anyone else's and loved to pray with you.

Jo, you not only got Mom's name, you got Mom's *friendliness*. Like her, you are simply unable to sit by a person and not strike up a conversation. You don't just talk to strangers ... give you ten minutes with anyone, and you will know their entire life history and secrets their own mother doesn't know about them. You have Mom's ability to engender immediate trust from people because, like Mom, you *genuinely care* about others. You also have the *"Best Mom"* trait that Mother demonstrated to us. You, like Mom, *are* that *mother bear*, and *nobody* better mess with your cubs! Jo, Mom loved you more than you will ever know—no matter what came about in these last few years. She cherished every Starbucks coffee you shared with her and every daily phone call. She depended on you to always be her *rock*, proof that "happily ever after" could truly be attained.

Taffy, even though you're not here, I believe all of us would agree that *you* received Mom's songwriting talent. We have featured one of your poems on the back of today's memorial service program. Mother would be so proud of you.

Me? I'd say I got Mom's work ethic too, but not to the extent Rodney has, some of her friendliness, but not as much as Jo has. Mostly, I inherited Mom's *love* of *animals*. *That* is the trait that I received in spades. I love them all, and like Mom, I believe my animals are just as important as any other member of my family.

I could tell so many stories of Mom rescuing animals or taking care of my pets. As a matter of fact, I *know* that my own 140-lb black lab, my beloved Samson, whom I had to let go in May at 14-plus years, well, he probably greeted Mom at the Pearly Gates, black tail wagging, because he will have recognized Mom as the one who taught me to *love all animals* with all my heart.

I also got Mom's ability to be creative with words—not with songwriting—but with my talent to write curriculum, lesson plans, and business documents. It has stood me well throughout my 30-year career as an educator.

Of all these gifts that Mom bestowed upon us, the *greatest gift* she gave to each of us, her four children, was *unconditional love*. She raised each of us to *love one another*. And we do! To this day, I absolutely *know*, without a doubt, that my brother and sister are my very best friends, the ones who will *always* be there for me, will rescue me if necessary, will forever support me. I hope they know the same is true about me for them.

We were never raised thinking of each other as "step" or "half" sister or brother, no matter our differing DNA. We *are family*! I simply can't think of any of you in any other way.

Suffice it to say that *each* of *us* in this room walked away the *better person* for having had Jo Buchanan touch our lives. We all have different memories of her. She had the ability to show different sides of her very complex and unique personality to each person she met, depending on *what* that particular person needed.

I want to close with this request: there are note cards in the back of the sanctuary on the small table. I ask that *each* of you take the time to write just a memory of what our mother meant to you, perhaps a story, perhaps your favorite memory of her, perhaps just your favorite thing about her that you'll miss. We would like to share these in future years to come with our own grandchildren who will never have the opportunity to know this *wonderful woman*, our *mother*, Sadie Jo Lowry Buchanan.

Thank you so very much for coming here today and honoring her memory with us.

Tribute to My Grandma Jo

By Derrick

When I think of my grandmother, I have many fond memories. The first thing that comes to mind is her scent. She always smelled amazing, like flowers and crisp leaves. Things like scents and sounds stick with you. I can still smell her sweet, ever-present scent. And her enthusiastic greeting, "Hi Derrick, how are you, son?"

I spent the most time with my grandmother during holidays when my parents would take me to visit family at her house in Altus. When you walked in, you could hear her Chow dogs barking in the distance. Grandma was a devout animal lover, and I think she passed that on to my mother and to me. I always remember her having dogs and cats.

And, Grandma was not a traditional gift-giver at the holidays. She always gave something that was funny and quirky, and even as a kid, I appreciated her sense of humor.

When I became an adult, I had the freedom to visit my grandma on my own, despite the 800 miles that separated her house from my parent's home in Alabama. Which brings me to perhaps my most cherished memory, of a time when I was able to spend quality one-on-one time with my grandma.

Upon a trip back to Alabama from my work out in the West, I always tried to stop in and visit family. Although I was perhaps only 20 years old, I had made a little money while working over the summer, and I was excited to treat my grandma to breakfast.

She met me at a restaurant just off my route. I felt proud to be on my own and taking my grandmother out to eat. She seemed proud too. She was genuinely excited to meet me and find out what was going on in my life, and share what was new in hers and my extended family's lives.

But, interestingly, every time she began telling me a story, another person walking by our booth at the restaurant would interrupt by saying hi to my grandmother. She seemed to know everyone. And, you could tell, they were genuinely excited to see her. Furthermore, she couldn't wait to introduce me as her grandson. I could tell she was proud, and I was so proud to be with her.

Upon my long drive home to Alabama, the rest of that day, I remember thinking about my grandmother's personality. She was caring, funny, and very likable. People wanted to be around her. She made them comfortable because they could tell that she cared. I'm honored to say that my grandmother had these qualities. And she left this world a better place.

Tribute to My Youngest Sister, Sadie Jo Lowry

By Fay Gatlin, Age 101, Dictated 11/2/2015

The first thing that comes to mind when I think of Sadie Jo is that she was always beautiful. She could get any boy she wanted, and she wanted them all! She had the boys waiting on her hand and foot.

Sadie Jo was the baby of the family, and she was always closer to Nerva Jewel than she was to me and Dollie because we were the oldest of the sisters. I was 14 when Sadie Jo was born. Dollie and me, we were married by the time Sadie Jo was in school. I know that Sadie Jo had Moma and Papa wrapped around her little finger—she could do no wrong as far as they were concerned.

Sadie Jo took care of Moma after Papa died. Moma stayed with Sadie Jo in Altus most of the time, and the rest of us kids didn't worry about her since we knew little sis was taking care of her. It was a blessing. I miss Moma and Papa, and I'm surely going to miss Sadie Jo. She's in a better place now.

Songs By My Mom

"You Looked the Other Way" by Jo Stout

Sung by Mary Kaye
Globe Recording Studio, Nashville, TN

I thought I'd forgotten the past
And, your love that didn't last
Then I happened to meet
You on the street
But You, looked the other way

You had someone new by your side
I felt sad; I could have cried
My heart stood still
With that old thrill
But you looked the other way

What did I do, so wrong,
I didn't dream, you'd be
So unforgiving and ashamed of me
I stopped you
But you wouldn't stay
So, I couldn't help but say
I must see you again
Oh please, please tell me when

But you looked the other way

I stopped you
but you wouldn't stay
So, I couldn't help but say
I must see you again
Please tell me when

But you looked the other way
Oh, you looked the other way

"Mommy Is Sleeping"

By Jo Stout

Mommy is sleeping
Don't make any noise
Little Sister, be quiet
Let's play with our toys

Though my heart was breaking
I happened to hear
Our sweet little darling
Whisper in her little sister's ear

Yes, Mommy is sleeping
She won't wake no more
Our Mommy, we love
The one we adore

Now let's be good, little sister
And when Mommy awakes
She will take us and love us
And make us a cake

My own heart was breaking
My darling lost her fight
You'll suffer no more
You're with God tonight

Yes, Mommy is sleeping
Don't make any noise
Little Sister, be quiet
Let's play with our toys

"Just an Old Wedding Custom"

By Jo Stout

Today I went to a wedding
I needed to attend
I couldn't help but think of
How different it might have been

It's an old wedding custom
To kiss the bride
But when I kissed my darling
My tears I had to hide

The mantle of rice I threw
At the Bride and groom
Just another old custom
To help hide my gloom

Just another old custom
For the Bride to cut the cake
But the love in my heart
I was too late

Just an old wedding custom
Good wishes and a handshake
But to lose the one you love
It's so hard to take

Just an old wedding custom
As the bells ring and play
The one I love married another
And broke my heart today

"I'm the Right Number, Baby"
By Jo Stout

I'm the right number, Baby
I'm all yours today
Quit shopping around, love
Cause I'm all yours today

I'm the right guy
For you and you're my doll
So let me tell you
Please give me a call

I'm the right number, Baby
When you get me on the line
I'm the right number, Baby
Please say you'll be mine

Just remember my number
And keep it in your heart
For you, I'm the right one
And I have been from the start

When the guys try to call you
Just hang up the phone
Remember my love
And Baby, come on home

I'm the right guy,
and Baby, you're my doll
So let me tell you
Please give me a call

I'm the right number Baby
When you get me on the line
I'm the right number Baby
Please say you'll be mine

I'm the right number Baby
Please say you'll be mine

Our Family

Figure 68 Mom's family at her memorial (I'm far right).

My Final Words

Unfinished Business

"Unfinished Business" by Katy Hurt

Although I made arrangements for my mother's interment shortly after her death, I still have my mother's ashes sitting on a counter (which freaks out my sister, Jo). No, this is not a guilt trip or some morbid fascination with the dead. This is the fulfillment of a promise I silently made to my mom after her death: I would find a way to honor her. By the time you read this, she will have been interred in a columbarium, along with a copy of this book. It is with a bit of humor that I bury my mother amongst a bunch of males, albeit monks and priests. I think she would have gotten a laugh out of that.

Another loose end was what exactly happened when my grandmother passed away, since she was such an integral part of our and my mother's life. Grandma died in 1979; I was married, teaching full-time, and living in another town when she passed. Supposedly, my grandmother died penniless with only the old homestead (and an uninhabitable concrete house) on virtually useless land in a flea-bitten town as her legacy. As worthless as it was, we all expected that it would go to my mom because she had been the one to house and support my grandmother for the past 20+ years. There were hard feelings among a few of her siblings (some of whom had not even seen my grandmother in 20+ years) who suddenly thought my mother had inherited a gold mine.

However, the worst of it was that my mom lied to my older brother and me; we were told there was no burial policy and that she needed money to bury my grandmother, at least until the property could be sold. So, my brother and I came up with about $700 each to help with Grandma's funeral. Turns out, the burial plot next to my grandfather had been paid for many years previous, and Mom had the old homestead sold before my grandmother turned cold. And, yes, there was indeed a small insurance policy, which could have paid for the funeral. It was definitely another instance of my mother omitting the truth; for what purpose, I can't say, because none of the money amounted to much—the insurance, the sale of Grandma's home, and even the cost of the funeral was nominal. It was one more mystery behind who Mom was and why she did what she did.

I know Mom missed Grandma. I know I did. She had always been a rock for us both for different reasons. Perhaps the downfall of my mother's life could have been averted had Grandma lived longer. She was the voice of reason many times during my youth; but, by 1979, she was well into her 90s and not in the best of health. I doubt Grandma carried much influence on my youngest sister, Taffy, who was hell-bent on destroying her life with drugs.

As for the rest of us, let me try to tie up some more of those loose ends. Despite my mother's marital examples, all four of us kids are doing fine … "fine" being a relative term. Three of us are happily married to life-long spouses, and one of us is happy to not be married. Of the three married, my sister, Jo, and brother, Rodney, married their high-school sweethearts (and both my in-laws are jewels). Although it took me a practice run of 21 years with my son's father, I can happily say I've found my forever spouse in Jimmy. *(Yes, Jeannie, he's a "Keeper!")*

Together, we have three kids (now, middle-aged adults) with their spouses, and seven grandkids. Life is good. Although I can take no credit for Jimmy's two, I think I did all right raising my own son, despite my not having a good parental role model; he values education as much as I do, got his Ph.D. in natural resources, and is a professor at a major university. Jimmy's daughter became a teacher (okay, maybe I did have a *little* influence because she was one of my students in high school), and his son has followed in his dad's footsteps, helping run Jimmy's business. We have no complaints about how our kids turned out, or their choice of spouses. We have been extremely blessed.

Taffy is another story. Hers will be a memoir worth writing one of these days; at the current time, it would be a tragedy, but I hope brighter days are ahead for my littlest sister. At the time of our mother's death, Taffy was in Arizona with, what I was told, a common-law husband. I knew the situation wasn't a good one, but I also knew I couldn't involve my own family, putting them at risk.

I offered to buy a bus ticket (she refused to fly) for my sister to come home for Mom's funeral. A back-and-forth negotiation ensued, in which she wanted me to send cash so she and her husband could rent a car and drive. I knew from past experience that I could not send money—it would be "stolen" or used for drugs, or God knows what. As a result, she did not attend. I did as she asked ... I saved a rose from Mom's funeral service and a program for her. I found out much later that her husband fully intended to cheat the cash out of me (not the first time) and never would have allowed her to leave.

255

Taffy had served her prison sentence and, for a short while, was on the road to recovery. However, the reappearance of her daughter, Candy, sealed her fate. Additional tangles with the law and drugs made her a fugitive for a time. According to Taffy herself, her own daughter (my niece) "sold her to a biker gang."

One of the bikers, Russell, claimed Taffy. He may have saved her life, but then again, he did not do so for any noble reason. She became his slave, literally, and punching bag. I hated getting the occasional call from my sister (when she could find a phone) to tell me of the latest abuse. They were never in one place for very long. I definitely offered to come get her, but she was too afraid, too beaten down. Taffy never once tried to extort money from me. I truly believe she was remorseful, but could see no way out of her situation. She was broken—body and soul.

For a short while, I thought things were headed in a good direction for my sister. She and Russell had moved back to Oklahoma, living on some land that belonged to his sister. I was finally able to send birthday cards, food, and even some occasional cash for Christmas and birthdays. I don't want to recount the number of times Taffy told me that "someone had stolen" her cards and money. So, instead, we started using money transfers through Walmart.

Regretfully, fairly recently, I got sucked in on what I now know was a scam. Taffy called and told me that she and Russell were about to lose the land they had lived on because his sister had not paid property taxes in years. Supposedly she and Russell had raised all but $1,000. I sent the money to her. When Taffy called to tell me they had been evicted anyway, I knew the truth of the situation. It wasn't long after this incident that Taffy contacted me to say she had finally left Russell. She now lives in a rental RV with her dogs. I never know exactly what to believe, but I pray she is happy and will someday find a better life. I fear that as long as she maintains contact with her daughter, this will never be the case.

As for Candy, my niece, she wound up going back to prison shortly after her incident with my mom in the nursing facility; this time, because of her age, it was the "real" prison, not juvie. I no longer accept her phone calls, because it was always one con after another ... "I may get early parole, so please send me money so I can buy some shoes for an interview," ... "I need a computer to work on my job skills," ... "I need to get this inmate off my back," ... and so on. I know these were scams because one of the calls was on a guard's phone. Whether the guard did this on purpose or not, I'll never know, but after we supposedly ended the call, I continued to hear my niece. She used horrible, filthy language, basically laughing at me and my credulity. I am gullible, but I do not want to be the enabler my mother was for these two. I now send only food and clothing to my sister, no cash.

Of my siblings, I am the only one who maintains contact with Taffy, and through her, my niece, Candy. Of course, we all love Taffy, and even Candy, but until their lives are straightened out, we cannot allow their situations and surroundings to affect us or the innocents in our families. We keep them in our prayers and continue to hope for better lives for each of them.

One last loose end: my mother's house fires need to be explained. (If I left any other dangling facts, please feel free to contact me so I can address those.) My family's first house fire occurred in Maryland before I started school, so sometime in the late '50s. We were not in base housing. I was told in later years, because I was too young to remember at the time, that it was dryer lint build-up that caused the fire. The worst thing about this whole ordeal was that we had two puppies who were in the basement; they died of smoke inhalation. None of us were there during the fire, having left for one of our very rare family outings. I only remember driving up to our street where fire trucks and police lights were on, being told that everything had been destroyed either by fire or water. I remember my mom crying and digging through rubble to find a pair of fancy shoes that had been dyed to match her dress; she and my dad were scheduled to attend some military event at the White House. To my knowledge, they didn't attend. We stayed in temporary base housing until permanent lodgings could be found.

To this day, I do not leave the dryer running when I leave my house. I am fanatic about always cleaning the lint after every load, even to the point of vacuuming the dryer itself and the outside vent hose every so often. It is surprising how many house fires start with the dryer. According to FEMA, failure to clean the dryer causes 34 percent of home fires.[6]

As unbelievable as it sounds, my mother suffered a second house fire in the late '70s in the home she had bought with Chick McGee. It was after her divorce from him but before her marriage to Buck Buchanan. My brother, sister, Jo, and I were all married and living in other towns.

---

[6] "Clothes Dryer Fire Safety Outreach Materials," U.S. Fire Administration, November 4, 2019, https://www.usfa.fema.gov/prevention/outreach/clothes_dryers.html.

The only ones living with my mom at that time were Taffy and Candy.

I received a call from my mother saying that her house had caught fire while she and the girls were visiting my Aunt Nerva Jewel in Texas. The fire department saved the house, but there was extensive smoke and water damage. Since no one was there, no one was injured. The house was refurbished, painted, and all new furniture was bought with the insurance money. During the renovation, my mom, sister, and niece stayed at the only motel in town, the Friendship Inn. We never learned the exact cause of the fire. My mom initially said it was faulty wiring. My brother heard it was a candle left burning in a bedroom. My sister, Jo, thought it had been a dryer fire again. Surprisingly, most of my mother's prized possessions, including a lot of her photos, were in a storage building in the backyard. You might be thinking as I did at the time; that the fire was possibly started on purpose. Since insurance paid, I would assume it was not arson, but the true cause will probably never be known.

Why did it take me seven years to write my mom's story, to get this book published? Answering that question would take a lot more self-knowledge than I possess. I wrote snippets here and there. I collected photos and bits of information every time I could, literally filling three huge boxes. To this day, a tidbit of information will be disclosed through a conversation with a sibling or even on a social post from a cousin. But the real reason it took so long was just life. Life carries on after the death of a loved one. I was still working full-time, and I was (and still am) actively involved with my grandkids.

Once I finally retired, I knew the time had come to put closure to this part of my life. Did I actively set out to "forgive" my mom? Did I purposely believe that writing a book would suddenly make me *like* my mother? No, to both these questions, but that is exactly what resulted once I started "getting to know" her. If there is one thing I've learned as a writer, you never know where the book is going to take you. If you listen, it takes on a life of its own and leads you where you are supposed to go.

If I left any other loose ends, please accept my apologies. A memoir is a difficult thing to write. The author bares the soul of not only herself, but also of her family. All the skeletons come out of the closet. There is constantly a niggling feeling of "What will so-and-so think if they read this?" However, the one thing my SPS (Self-Publishing School) coaches stressed for a memoir was: be honest. So I have tried to tell the truth, no matter how painful. I hope I have not offended anyone. But most of all, I pray I have given my mother the respect, honor, and admiration I failed to give her while she was alive. If Mom is reading this from heaven, I hope she laughs at her antics, forgives my disclosing family secrets, and knows with her entire being that I love and *like* her with all my heart and soul.

Thank You for Reading

How I Learned to Like My Mom!

Whether you bought this for yourself or received it as a gift, I hope you were entertained and learned a lesson or two … even if it was only to clean out the dryer vent.

Seriously, regardless of why you read my book, I hope it encourages you to rebuild any relationships you may have, to unconditionally forgive any wrongs that have been done to you, and most of all, to *love* everyone without judgment. Wouldn't the entire world be a better place if each and every one of us could do this?

I welcome your feedback and would most sincerely appreciate you sharing your thoughts in a review on Amazon, especially if it's a 5-star review! Your input is invaluable to me as an author.

Thank you!

Let's connect! I look forward to hearing from you!

Website: www.PullUpYourBootstraps.org.
Email: dorenda@PullUpYourBootstraps.org.

Don't forget your free gift! *Want an insider's view of life with my Grandma? How about a taste of her Homemade Yeast Rolls? Please visit my website at the above address to get "**Grandma**," my short story featuring my Grandma at her best AND a copy of her recipe for yeast rolls.*

Blessings,

Dorenda Doyle

Acknowledgments

I have so many to thank, not just for this book but for my sanity and survival through these many years. However, I give thanks to God first and foremost. I have always believed that He has His hand on my life, that He has always brought me through every test and fire a better person. Despite difficulties, I absolutely know He has gifted me with a charmed life. It is my strongest belief that "everything happens for a reason."

If I go in chronological order of whom to thank, of course, Grandma is top of the list; she protected me, guided me, and was the best role model ever. My brother, Rodney, and my sister, Jo, are there too. Rodney—I am so glad your memory, and that of your wife, Terri, are superior to my own; many of the stories in this book are so much better because of your input. Rodney was my encourager to keep writing, to get it done; love you, Big Brother. Jo, my sister and best friend in the whole world, encouraged me early on to write this book, to find my own healing by getting things on paper; thank you, Dear Sister.

My son, Derrick, has always been my biggest advocate—I don't know if you are just being encouraging, Kiddo, or if you truly believe I'm as capable as you always seem to think. Thanks to him and my daughter-in-law, Patricia, for always being there for me. Their daughter, Appleton, makes me feel like I can conquer the world; I hope I am always her hero, just as Grandma was mine.

The past 25+ years have been some of my happiest, thanks to the man I adore, Jimmy, and the family he has brought into my life—two more kids (Trey and Lindsey), their spouses (Heather and Nathan), and my mom-in-law, Cathy.

Ultimately, our seven amazing, adorable, and awesome grandkids (Maddie, Ty, Bentlie, Libby, Appleton, Letty, and Loxley) make our lives complete. I'm even lucky enough to have a bonus grandkid (Magnolia). Grandkids, dogs, and a cat—I could not have dreamed or designed a better life for myself.

I was told by the *best* editor in the entire world, Jeannie Culbertson, that I should acknowledge any and all who helped make this book possible. That would not be complete without recognizing my best friends. I am fortunate enough to have two more besties besides my sister, Jo. Jane Frutiger was not only my beta reader but was on constant standby to hear one idea after another, look at photos, talk me off the ledge, and share advice. Deborah Westerfield was the first to suggest that my title be a positive one; she consistently reminded me to honor my mom, not just tell a story. Both these women shore me up, and my life is so much better with you both in it.

Two more women who have been my cheering squad for more than 35+ years are Linda Bearse and Debbie Marcus; your shoulders for tears and advice for my ears have been invaluable. You are truly sisters of my heart.

My Saint Bernard family—Abbot Marcus Voss, OSB, Sr. Marian Davis, OSB, Joyce Nix, and Carolyn Branch—I hope you know how much you have meant to me over the years; you believed in me when I didn't believe in myself.

Friendships, whether at work or at play, are so very important to one's self-worth, so never take them for granted. I am the better person for having had the friendships of Dr. Sylvia Gist, Marlene Green, and Kathy

Miller. A special shout-out to my friend Lina Benedetti who is always ready for a biking, hiking, or whatever adventure!

Heartfelt thanks and love to my TN cousins Sharrell, Bill, Terri, Tony, Grady, and Charlotte, and my TX cousins Nerva Jo, Jean, and Darlene—you have all been inspirations, shared photos and stories, and make me proud to claim our Lowry heritage. I regret any pain this story brings to any member of my family, especially my youngest sister, Taffy. I love you all.

The biggest reason you are able to enjoy this book is because of an entity called SPS, Self-Publishing School. Without the guidance of this course and its instructors, I never would have known how to bring my story to the light. Thank you, thank you, thank you. (And, if you have a story to tell, please check them out!)

I appreciate all the support staff that helped birth this book—fellow authors Ralph Koerber, Tracy Bittner, Mark Reznick, Jenny Schiffner (Jen Telger), and Dawn Cuckow, my photographer, Lisa Jones of Cullman, AL, my SPS coaches, Barbara Hertzler and Michele Gano, and most importantly, Jeannie Culbertson ~The NoteworthyMom, for her guidance and suggestions with my book. Jeannie, your kind advice and encouragement have helped me more than you may ever know, and I have a feeling this is just the beginning of our friendship.

Lastly, thank you, Mom. I always loved you. Not that you need to hear it now, but I do indeed like you. I admire you. I respect you. Truth be told, I probably always did, but was too immature to admit it ...

About the Author

Dorenda is a retired educator of thirty years, having taught business and computers at high school and college levels, writing curriculum for two state education departments and serving in administrative roles. (M.Ed., Secondary Education; B.S., Business Management.) She was even a zoo docent (volunteer educator) for a few years at the Birmingham Zoo.

Since retirement, her zeal for education has been replaced with a passion for grandkids, animals, and travel. With three rescues of her own (Shadow, Murphy, and Taco), she supports and advocates for animal rescue in her spare time.

Her photography hobby almost always includes pictures of grandkids and animals, usually together. Biking and hiking take up the rest of her free time, with week-long bicycling trips being a yearly indulgence. Her bucket list includes visiting all 63 National Parks and biking a "century" (100 miles in one day; so far, 77 is her best).

In addition, she and her husband, Jimmy, travel as much as possible with the entire extended family of sixteen, including her 91-year-young mom-in-law. It's these adventures on which she will base her future books, a children's series, *Adventures With Grandma*.

www.ingramcontent.com/pod-product-compliance
Lightning Source LLC
Chambersburg PA
CBHW060906120626
46553CB00001B/227